Cognitive Behavioural Therapy

7 Ways to Freedom from Anxiety, Depression, and Intrusive Thoughts!

Table of Contents

Understanding Cognitive Behavioural Therapy

We are what we think.
All that we are arises with our thoughts.
With our thoughts we make the world.
—Buddha

Millennia before cognitive behavioural therapy, the Buddha emphasized the power of thought for shaping feelings, actions, and lives. This concept has echoes in most major religions of the world. The Christian tradition has *metanoia*, which translates as "changing your mind / how you think". In Jewish tradition, there's King Solomon's saying "For as he thinks in his heart, so is he". And in Islam, this verse from Qur'an: "Surely Allah does not change the condition of a people until they change their own condition."

The concept of thought as the basis of feeling is also reflected in modern psychology. It is at the core of cognitive behavioural therapy (CBT), which helps patients change the way they feel by changing the way they think. CBT draws heavily on mindfulness techniques and other ways of "thinking about thinking" developed by Eastern philosophy.

What is Cognitive Behavioural Therapy?

We can't always change our circumstances or the situations that life hands us, but we can change how we think about them—and thus, how we feel about them. This is the basic theory behind CBT.

CBT is a research-based treatment approach for mood and anxiety disorders that combines both cognitive and behavioural methods. It has strong support in the scientific literature as an effective treatment for depression, anxiety, eating disorders, and other conditions. The central assertion of CBT is that situations are viewed through cognitive frameworks that lead to specific thoughts. These thoughts lead to feelings. Feelings can be pleasant or unpleasant; in the case of anxiety and mood disorders, therapy usually addresses unpleasant feelings of distress, fear, or hopelessness. Since feelings are often difficult to change directly, CBT focuses on changing the thoughts and behaviors that lead to these feelings. Its premise is simple: By being mindful of your thoughts, you can control your feelings and, consequently, your actions. This helps you manage your life more effectively, develop a positive outlook, and maintain constructive behavior patterns.

CBT was developed in the 1950s and 1960s by psychologists Albert Ellis and Aaron T. Beck. Dr. Ellis had originally been a proponent of classical psychoanalysis but lost faith in the method over time. Influenced by ancient and modern philosophy, especially Stoicism, Ellis created a new form of therapy that focused on helping patients understand their own irrational beliefs and restructure those that lead to emotional pain and suffering. This approach became known as Rational Emotive Behavioural Therapy (REBT) and bears many similarities to CBT.

Dr. Aaron Beck helped conduct research to support this new concept of "cognitive therapy." He is considered the founder of cognitive behavioral therapy, which combines the cognitive restructuring elements with behavioral modification. He also explained how dysfunctional thinking could lead to psychological problems. Beck too had been a supporter of classical psychoanalytic theories but began looking for new approaches when his experiments failed to validate those concepts. Like Ellis, he found that actively engaging patients in the process of identifying negative thoughts helped them develop more rational belief systems and overcome mental illnesses such as depression.

Ultimately, Beck and Ellis both asserted that thoughts and beliefs are empirically testable hypotheses. Thus, if a client was suffering from depression or anxiety rooted in irrational beliefs, the condition could be greatly improved by the client's collaborating with a therapist to identify the beliefs, challenge them, and form new, more reasonable beliefs and thinking patterns. This method of cognitive therapy differs profoundly from older models of psychoanalysis. Psychoanalysts did little to engage their patients, who had a mostly passive role. Often, attention was focused on discovering the root of the problem and did not necessarily change thought patterns or behavior to counter it. Cognitive behavioral therapists avoid this approach.

When working with a patient, CBT-based therapists aim to help build a set of skills that can be developed, practiced, and applied outside the therapy sessions. This aspect, which may include readings and at-home exercises, makes CBT different from other therapies that focus on discussing problems and offering advice during visits. These skills include having an awareness of thoughts and emotions and being able to identify how different situations influence thoughts and behaviors, how thoughts and behaviors effect emotions, and ultimately, how dysfunctional thoughts and behaviors can be modified in ways that lead to more pleasant and manageable feelings.

What Is CBT For?

Cognitive behavioural therapy can be helpful for a wide range of mental disorders, including anxiety, depression, some phobias, and coping with severe illness or death. Many people suffer from one or more of these things at some point in their lives, and CBT is a useful approach to addressing them, either alone or with a therapist.

Understanding Anxiety

Anxiety is a normal emotion, but it can get out of control. It helps us in physically dangerous situations by activating a part of the automatic nervous system and preparing the body for fighting or running away. The automatic nervous system controls all our involuntary activities, like breathing, heartbeat, and digestion. It has two components, the sympathetic and the parasympathetic nervous systems. The sympathetic nervous system can be thought of as a gas pedal. It triggers the fight-or-flight response, resulting in faster breathing and heart rate, the release of adrenaline and other stress hormones, and a spike in blood glucose levels. This would have saved our lives many times in the past, but these days, it is frequently activated in response to situations that aren't actually physically threatening, like traffic jams, work presentations, or arguments with a spouse. Worse, it stays activated when stress levels stay high, causing actual physical damage to our bodies including inflammation, high blood pressure, and a higher risk of heart disease. It also leads to symptoms that make day-to-day life more difficult and less enjoyable including insomnia, a sense of dread, irritability, restlessness, poor concentration, sweating, and feeling on edge.

The good thing is that we can stop this physiological cascade of stress responses by doing things that activate the parasympathetic nervous system. The parasympathetic nervous system is like the brake pedal. It is activated when the brain receives messages that it is safe to relax, resulting in slower heart rate and breathing, a drop in stress-hormone levels, and improved digestion. Many things increase parasympathetic nervous system activity, including deep breathing, mantra meditation, yoga, repetitive prayer, tai chi, being in nature, visualizing calm scenes, and being with supportive friends or loved ones. CBT can help by changing the pattern of thoughts and underlying beliefs that lead to an anxious emotional and physical state and by encouraging activities that reduce stress. It can also help by changing avoidance behaviors and maladaptive coping mechanisms.

Cognitive behavioral therapy is effective for addressing depression and low-mood disorders as well. With these disorders, people tend to have negative thoughts about themselves and the future. They may feel hopeless or worthless and think that others do not like them. These disorders are linked with genetics and other biological factors, as well as childhood experiences, life stressors, and traumatic events. When people have low mood or depression, they may avoid activities and events. They may experience a wide range of symptoms, including feelings of sadness, guilt, isolation, or numbness, lack of confidence, self-loathing, trouble sleeping, lack of energy, altered appetite, lack of concentration, and thoughts of suicide or self-harm. CBT can help by challenging the negative thought patterns and underlying beliefs that lead to these kinds of emotions. As with anxiety, CBT can also help change problematic behaviors associated with depression and low mood.

However, CBT is not appropriate for all issues, and in some cases, it should not be attempted alone. If the condition involves substance abuse, self-harm, suicidal thoughts, thoughts of causing harm to others, personality disorders, or severe psychiatric conditions, it's important to seek help from a trained therapist.

Understanding the Cognitive Behavioural Model

Before beginning CBT, it's important to understand the cognitive model, a theory used in psychology to explain how behaviors, thoughts, and feelings are related. Often, people believe that their feelings result from a situation—for example, "I did not do well on a work or school presentation" → "I feel worthless." Yet many people experience that same situation and react in ways that don't include feeling worthless, even though they might feel frustrated or disappointed. Something beyond the situation itself effects how we feel.

The cognitive model challenges the idea of a direct connection between situations or experiences and feelings and posits that it is actually the thoughts we have about those situations that result in the feelings we have. Indeed, people with depression or anxiety tend to have thinking patterns that are dysfunctional and inaccurate. For example, the individual who does one presentation poorly and feels worthless is responding not so much to the situation but to the inaccurate thoughts that result from that situation, such as "You can't do anything right" or "You always mess things up," which are unfair and exaggerated assessments of reality.

CBT teaches people suffering from unpleasant or

upsetting feelings to challenge the thoughts and beliefs that lead to those feelings. This is important because rather than encouraging you to avoid situations that lead to these feelings (which may be impossible), CBT helps you learn how to change your thoughts about a situation in a way that changes the feelings that result from it. This is the cognitive aspect of cognitive behavioral therapy. The behavioral aspect of CBT deals with how different behaviors influence mood. It aims to teach clients to increase behaviors associated with a positive mood and avoid behaviors associated with a negative mood.

Cognitive theory outlines three levels of thoughts and beliefs: automatic thoughts, assumptions, and core beliefs. All three levels can be dysfunctional to varying degrees. The first level, automatic thoughts, can be viewed as the stream-of-consciousness type of thoughts about ourselves and others that pop into our minds throughout the day. They are usually situation specific, and we may or may not be aware of them, though we often feel the emotions that result from them. Often, automatic thoughts overestimate threats and underestimate our ability to deal with problems. Sometimes they become distorted, but we continue to accept them as true. These thoughts are the result of dysfunctional beliefs about ourselves, others, and the world, and they can be exaggerated by depression or anxiety.

These thoughts can be identified, challenged, and replaced with more reasonable thoughts.

The second level, known as intermediate beliefs or assumptions, consists of views about the world that are less situation specific than automatic thoughts. They are essentially a type of rule or generalization that individuals develop as they process and categorize the patterns and information around them. These beliefs shape thoughts, which then influence behavior. Like automatic thoughts, assumptions can become distorted. For example, "If I am successful in the business world, I will be loved" and "If I do not make myself more physically attractive, I will never find a spouse" are dysfunctional assumptions.

Finally, core beliefs are foundational beliefs about the world that we usually form in childhood. These are reinforced throughout life by our perceptions. They are generalized and absolute, though they can be completely false. People tend to focus on new information that confirms existing beliefs and ignore information that contradicts them, making core beliefs hard to change. Negative and dysfunctional core beliefs can act as drivers for dysfunctional assumptions and negative thoughts. For example, a core belief that "I'm unlovable" may lead to assumptions about the success or appearance needed to ensure love from others. Core beliefs often relate to achievement and relationships with others. Assumptions and core beliefs can be challenged and altered with a similar approach to automatic thoughts.

The relationship between core beliefs, assumptions, automatic thoughts, and emotions can be summarized as follows: core beliefs → assumptions → automatic thoughts (generated by a situation) → emotions. Another way to think about it is with the ABC model, which stands for **a**ctivating event, **b**eliefs and thoughts, and emotional and behavioral **c**onsequences. The "A-B-C" sequence represents the fact that an event or situation merely activates a series of thoughts; it does not cause feelings. The thoughts and beliefs we have are what cause the feelings. This is great news, because while we cannot always change situations and events, *we can change what we think and believe*.

As you begin working through CBT, the first step will be learning to identify dysfunctional automatic thoughts. Once you can identify them, you can challenge these thoughts, which can result in almost-immediate improvements in feelings. Then, you can begin to identify the assumptions and core beliefs that underlie these harmful thought patterns. Ideally, CBT will help you reexamine and change the assumptions and core beliefs that contribute to dysfunctional thoughts and the upsetting feelings that result from them.

Making CBT Effective

The attitude and approach you bring to CBT will have a big impact on your success. Having a positive attitude is important. People who believe that this approach may benefit them are more likely to experience positive outcomes than people who begin with the belief that nothing will help them. It also helps to have a strong motivation to change.

Clear goals are central to the CBT process. CBT works best for specific problems, fears, or patterns of thinking, so having a focused plan for what you hope to get out of it is likely to make it more effective. Having clear goals will also enable you to realize when you aren't making progress, so you can adjust your activities, your plan, or the goals themselves.

Cognitive behavioural therapy requires you to put in time to practice the skills you have learned, including working independently on readings, filling out thought journals, reflecting on obstacles and goals, and facing anxiety-producing situations. It is an active, engaged process. If you do not dedicate time to the suggested activities, it will likely be of little help.

While you should encourage yourself to complete the reflections and activities, be kind, respectful, nonjudgmental, honest, and accepting with yourself no matter what you do. Always validate your experience. No matter how others perceive you or how you perceive yourself for feeling a certain way, those feelings are real, and they affect your quality of life. You don't have to justify yourself. You are seeking change in your life because in some way or another, you have been suffering. You have taken a step toward that goal, and that is an accomplishment.

A key aspect of the CBT process is the thought journal. You will use it to write down the problem, goals, and obstacles at the beginning of the process, and throughout the process to identify, evaluate, and challenge negative thoughts. Consistently using the thought journal is essential, because CBT is based on your direct engagement in the healing process. However, as you become familiar with the thinking exercises, you can do some of them in your head.

Monitoring Progress

As you work through the CBT process, keep track of your progress, as measured by mood, engagement in activities, and achievement of stated goals. Use the table included in the workbook, and fill out the columns for mood and intensity, behavioral-activation activities you did, and what you did that day that helped move you toward your goal.

If you don't see improvement right away, that's OK. It may take a week or two to see changes. However, you may need to make some adjustments. You may need to redefine goals, if you find that the ones you stated are either not that important to you or more impractical than you thought. You may need to choose behavioral-activation activities that you are more likely to complete or that are more interesting to you. You may need to spend more time working on the thought journal and identifying and challenging automatic thoughts. Or you may need to look again at the obstacles you listed and see whether they are slowing progress.

Some difficulty is OK, since challenging yourself is a part of growth. But CBT is a gentle approach that should not result in any kind of extreme discomfort or severe symptoms, especially when you are working on your own. If this occurs, discontinue that particular activity, discontinue self-directed CBT as a whole, if needed, or seek the advice of a professional therapist. Let's begin!

Cognitive Behavioural Therapy (*in Seven Steps*)

Step 1: Identifying The Problem

The first step in the cognitive behavioral therapy process is identifying a problem to work on. It can be a behavior that you would like to change, an unpleasant feeling you often have, or a type of upsetting thought. Below, we will discuss dysfunctional automatic thoughts and intrusive thoughts, two common types of unwanted thoughts that can be addressed with CBT. Since they are so common, and since they are symptoms of other disorders, including post-traumatic stress disorder, generalized anxiety disorder, obsessive-compulsive disorder, eating disorders, and depression, it's a good idea to know more about them. If you are suffering with either of these types of thoughts, you'll be better equipped to identify them. Then, we will explain how to describe the problem in detail so that you can begin addressing it.

What Are Automatic Thoughts?

Automatic thoughts are a central aspect of the CBT theory. Automatic thoughts are those that come into our minds quickly, without effort. They are short and related to the specific situation at hand. They occur during or right after the situation, as an "instinctive" response. They don't include reflection or careful logic but usually seem quite reasonable. Some are perfectly logical; others are known as "dysfunctional automatic thoughts."

Recognizing dysfunctional automatic thoughts is an important skill to develop in the CBT process. You can begin by noticing when a certain thought seems to trigger a negative emotion. Pay special attention to thoughts that lead to a fast change in mood, since they are often linked to dysfunctional core beliefs. For example, you might be watching a video of someone—a scientist, an entrepreneur, or a politician—giving a talk that is met with applause and laughter by the audience. You might think, "I will never be popular like that," or "No one thinks I'm funny," or "That person is so much happier than I am." These are dysfunctional automatic thoughts.

Once you have focused on a situation in which you experienced negative emotions, you can ask yourself some questions to try to pinpoint what types of thoughts and beliefs trigger the feelings you wish to change.

1. What was I doing right before I felt like that?
2. Where was I when I felt like that? Are there places where I never have those feelings?
3. How was I acting just beforehand?

4. What was I thinking about before those feelings started?
5. Are there certain beliefs I hold that seem to increase those feelings?
6. Whom was I with when I felt like that? Do I feel like that with everyone?

For example, some people may feel sad and hopeless in relation to a fear that they will be alone their whole lives. Focusing on that situation, you could notice the fact that this feeling might arise more often when home alone late at night, but rarely feel this way when spending time with friends. You might realize that you think things like "I will never find a girlfriend/boyfriend" based on negative beliefs about your desirability as a partner.

Another example is people struggling with negative thoughts about body image and desires for extreme weight loss. You might notice that after going to the gym or reading fashion magazines, you feel more concerned about body size. Analyzing this situation, you realize that automatic thoughts such as "Those people are happier than I am," "My thighs are too big," and "Everyone thinks I eat too much" trigger a flood of negative emotions. You also realize that these thoughts are based on the incorrect assumptions "Skinny people are much happier" and "That is how a man's/woman's body is supposed to look." Digging deeper, you may even realize that all this is based on a dysfunctional core belief that happiness requires perfection.

Most people are surprised to realize how many automatic thoughts pass through their minds in a matter of seconds. Once you become aware of them, you can approach a thought in several ways. If you feel that a particular thought is representative of the larger issue, you can focus on that thought. If you feel that another thought better connects to the problem, you can focus on that instead. Or if you feel that the issue underlying that particular automatic thought is not as important as other issues, you can set it aside and focus on other thoughts that had a stronger impact on your mood. When evaluating a series of automatic thoughts, assess how intense the feelings they stimulated were, and choose the thoughts that had the biggest impact.

Often, these types of dysfunctional thoughts result from cognitive distortions, or "thought traps," which are essentially mistakes we make in the thinking process. Automatic thoughts tend to fall into a few categories of cognitive distortions. Identifying the general patterns can be helpful in changing the thoughts that are a part of that pattern. It may be helpful to write down some of your automatic thoughts and then look for patterns. Below, we list some common types of cognitive distortions. Noting down what types of cognitive distortions you tend to make can help you identify your dysfunctional automatic thoughts.

Catastrophizing. Predicting extremely negative future outcomes, such as “If I don’t do well on this paper, I will flunk out of college and never have a good job.”

All-or-nothing. Viewing things as all-good or all-bad, black or white, as in “If my new colleagues don’t like me, they must hate me.”

Personalization. Thinking that negative actions or words of others are related to you, or assuming that you are the cause of a negative event when you actually had no connection with it.

Overgeneralizations. Seeing one negative situation as representative of all similar events.

Labeling. Attaching negative labels to ourselves or others. Rather than focusing on a particular thing that you didn’t like and want to change, you might label yourself a loser or a failure.

Magnification/minimization. Emphasizing bad things and deemphasizing good in a situation, such as making a big deal about making a mistake, and ignoring achievements.

Emotional reasoning. Letting your feelings about something guide your conclusions about how things really are, as in "I feel hopeless, so my situation really must be hopeless.'"

Discounting positives. Disqualifying positive experiences as evidence that your negative beliefs are false—for example, by saying that you got lucky, something good happened accidentally, or someone was lying when giving you a compliment.

Negativity bias. Seeing only the bad aspects of a situation and dwelling on them, in the process viewing the situation as completely bad even though there may have been positives.

Should/must statements. Setting up expectations for yourself based on what you think you "should" do. These usually come from perceptions of what others think, and may be totally unrealistic. You might feel guilty for failing or not wanting these standards and feel frustration and resentment. Buddhism sets this in context. When the word "should" is used, it leaves no leeway for flexibility of self-acceptance. It is fine to have wise, loving, self-identified guidelines for behavior, but remember that the same response or action to all situations is neither productive nor ideal. One size never fits all.

Jumping to conclusions. Making negative predictions about the outcome of a situation without definite facts or evidence. This includes predicting a bad future event and acting as if it were already fact, or concluding that others reacted negatively to you without asking them.

Dysfunctional automatic thoughts like these are common. If you think that they are causing suffering in your life, make sure you address them as a part of your CBT focus.

What Are Intrusive Thoughts?

Intrusive thoughts are another type of common but upsetting thought. Our brains generate many thoughts and ideas over the course of a day. Some feel completely normal, productive, and helpful, and we view them as reflective of who we are. Some thoughts may strike us as odd or confusing but are easily dismissed and don't cause much distress. We can also experience thoughts that seem bad, scary, or sickening—things that don't fit with who we are or that make us feel terrible, yet are hard to get rid of. These are known as intrusive thoughts.

Intrusive thoughts are thoughts, ideas, or impulses that are unwanted and upsetting but continue to occur. They are difficult to stop or control, which often makes them more distressing. They may interrupt activities and thought processes and cause feelings of doubt, shame, guilt, confusion, fear, and anxiety. Intrusive thoughts are common symptoms of anxiety disorders, obsessive-compulsive disorder (OCD), and post-traumatic stress disorder, but they can occur independently as well.

There are several types of intrusive thoughts, which may be treated in different ways. Obsessional intrusions usually relate to something that a person finds upsetting, disgusting, or repugnant, such as violence, taboo sexual acts, or his or her religious beliefs. These are often addressed within an OCD framework. Worry intrusions are anxious thoughts about future events or threats. Usually, dealing with anxiety through a range of CBT techniques will help reduce the frequency and severity of worry intrusions. Trauma-related intrusions are sudden recollections of past traumatic events. Addressing the feelings around these events with a therapist may help.

Trauma-related intrusions are sudden recollections of past traumatic events. Addressing the feelings around this event with a therapist may help.

Examples of Intrusive Thoughts:

- Unwanted sexual thoughts involving a family member, child, or animal (obsessional intrusion)
- Unwanted sexual thoughts involving a coworker whom you are not attracted to (obsessional intrusion)
- Thoughts of committing a crime or violent act that you know you would never do, such as killing your spouse or harming your baby (obsessional intrusion)
- Fear that you won't be able to stop yourself from saying something inappropriate in public (obsessional intrusion)
- Worries that you no longer believe in your religion, briefly thought something forbidden, or performed a ritual incorrectly (obsessional intrusion)
- Repeated, intensely felt doubts about your ability to perform on an upcoming exam you have studied for (worry intrusion)

- Recurrent, distressing thoughts about contracting a rare disease and dying (worry intrusion)
- Repeated thoughts about a humiliating event that happened in childhood (trauma-related intrusion)
- Unwanted, upsetting recollections of a violent event you experienced as an adult (trauma-related)

These are just some of the many forms that intrusive thoughts can take. Many people are surprised to realize that others have experienced similar types of intrusive thoughts. Knowing this can be reassuring and help you reach a better understanding of intrusive thoughts as a common phenomenon, not a uniquely personal illness or failing.

Intrusive thoughts are common. In a study titled "You Can Run but You Can't Hide: Intrusive Thoughts on Six Continents" and published in the *Journal of Obsessive-Compulsive and Related Disorders*, researchers asked people in thirteen countries on six continents questions about experiencing intrusive thoughts. The authors found that on average, 94 percent of people around the world experience intrusive thoughts at least occasionally. If this finding held up to further testing, the authors concluded, the implication would be "that intrusions are a normal and ubiquitous aspect of human cognition" (Radomsky et al. 2013).

Almost everyone has intrusive thoughts, but people

respond to them in different ways. The key difference between people who do not struggle with their intrusive thoughts and those who do is not that the former do not have them, though they may experience them less frequently or intensely, but that they are able to dismiss upsetting, unwanted thoughts as meaningless. Those who struggle with obsessive thoughts tend to attach great significance to the thoughts and conclude that they really do believe or feel those things or really will commit those acts. They begin to build a narrative around the thoughts, with implications about their own character, behavior, and future actions.

The most important thing to understand about intrusive thoughts is that just having a certain thought or image *does not mean it is true.* Having an intrusive thought about an unacceptable violent or sexual action doesn't mean you actually want to or will commit the act. If you are religious, having a distressing blasphemous thought doesn't mean you truly believe it. Experiencing recurrent anxious thoughts about a future event does not mean that those fears are well founded or that the bad outcome is likely to occur.

Steven Phillipson, PHD, is a true expert in the field. He reminds his patients that they are not "mentally ill". Instead, they simply have an anxiety disorder. He also prefers to call intrusive thoughts "creative associations." This attitude encourages patients to fully embrace their experience of these common, if sometimes disturbing, thoughts. Find out more by searching "Dr. Phillipson OCD" in YouTube.

If intrusive thoughts are causing you distress, include them in the description of your problem. In Step 4, we will discuss a variety of ways to deal with intrusive thoughts using CBT-based techniques.

Describing the Problem

Now, make a list of the most important problems or concerns you'd like to address. Note how often they occur, whether they are relatively minor or quite severe, and how they impact your life. Use the workbook in the appendix at the end of this book.

For example, someone may experience feelings of hopelessness. To address this, you could write down that these thoughts occur three to four days a week, that the thoughts are upsetting and intrusive but not so severe that you cannot continue most daily activities, and the impact is that the thoughts take away from your enjoyment of life and make you feel less positive about the future in general. Another example is someone suffering from severe anxiety. We might experience these anxious feelings on a daily basis, feel them intensely, and as a result, have trouble sleeping, concentrating at work, maintaining relationships, and enjoying leisure activities. Problems can also be more concrete than feelings. For example, you could pinpoint overeating in response to stress from work, or smoking cigarettes as the problem you would like to resolve.

Step 2: Setting Goals

Now that you've identified the major issue, you can set goals for what you hope to achieve with CBT. Goals should be specific, measurable, and achievable. In other words, focus on the changes that would be really meaningful to you to achieve within the next few weeks or months, and think about how you will know when you have achieved those changes. For example, avoid setting goals like "Feel less depressed" or "Stop feeling worried." Instead, state what you want to feel more of ("Feel more energetic, hopeful, and so on") as well as what that would look like to you, such as "Get up early three to four mornings each week feeling happier" and "Do leisure activities that I enjoy three days each week." Goals could also relate to facing situations that cause anxiety ("Beginning in two weeks, speak up in class/meetings three to four times per week") or intrusive thoughts ("Reduce the distress associated with intrusive thoughts by half").

Avoid setting goals that require big, immediate changes or doing something every single day. If you are trying to begin exercising to improve mood and overall health, start by aiming for a thirty-minute walk four times per week, rather than running for one hour every day.

Unreasonable goals can create a sense of failure when you don't achieve them right away. If you wish, you can set goals for the short, medium, and long term that reflect both reasonable expectations for the present and high hopes for the future. You can set long-term goals as far out as a few years into the future, but make sure you have achievable goals in the next few weeks as well.

It may be helpful to identify broad areas, such as family, health, and work, and then identify specific goals within those areas. You may also wish to prioritize your goals and start by focusing on those you feel are most important or most achievable. Make sure any goal you set is truly meaningful to *you*. If you realize that one of your goals doesn't feel important, try refining it or discarding it all together.

Whether you're struggling with negative self-image, social anxiety and/or an avoidance of group activities you used to enjoy, two goals might be 1) to develop a more balanced view of yourself and trust in your ability to positively interact with others, and 2) to start attending social events again or to commit yourself to a regular social activity.

Once you have outlined your goals, it is important to describe what steps are needed to reach them in concrete terms. For someone with social anxiety, for example, the steps might look something like this:

- Learn two strategies to challenge negative self-talk.
- Use online resources to learn two strategies to handle difficult social situations.
- Reengage in two of the clubs I was in over the next two months.

In the workbook in the appendix, write down your goals as specifically as possible, including a time frame.

Step 3: Identifying Obstacles

As you get started, it can also be useful to identify things that could get in the way of the cognitive behavioral therapy process. Challenges could include lack of support from family, friend groups that support maladaptive or harmful behavior, financial issues that relate to the problem, or belief systems that conflict with the desired outcome. Challenges could also be practical things, such as traffic that makes it difficult to get to an event. Common challenges people face include worries about doing things perfectly, to the point where they continue to avoid taking action on their goals, being constantly busy and not devoting sufficient time and effort to applying CBT techniques, and feeling discouraged and giving up if there is not improvement right away.

All these things are normal responses to the challenge of addressing difficult emotions. For many people, the first phase will feel the most difficult, like getting up the steep part of a hill before it levels out to a gentler incline. It's important to devote the time you deserve to heal your mind from negative thoughts and feelings. Try to maintain a positive attitude, even if you don't feel changes right away. Don't worry about doing anything perfectly, and congratulate yourself when you take any steps toward your goal. There are no failures, only opportunities to learn from tasks that were harder than expected. It's all part of the process.

Think about what might be difficult for you, and then write down two to three things you can do to prevent, avoid, or overcome those obstacles. For example, finding twenty minutes per day writing down automatic thoughts and challenging intermediate beliefs might be hard. You could set a specific time each day, create a backup opportunity, such as doing some reflection instead of watching a certain TV show, or ask a friend or partner to sit with you for twenty minutes each day while you write. In the workbook in the appendix, write down several possible obstacles and the strategies you can use to overcome them.

Step 4: Challenging Automatic and Intrusive Thoughts

In Step 1, we explained how to identify dysfunctional automatic thoughts and intrusive thoughts, common problems that can be addressed with CBT. In Step 4, we will look at ways to challenge and change those thought patterns.

Challenging Dysfunctional Automatic Thoughts

The process of challenging maladaptive thoughts and beliefs begins with automatic thoughts. Thoughts that lead to anxiety, depression, and phobias are often extreme and unrealistic. But people dealing with these conditions may have a hard time separating real from exaggerated statements. As we discussed above, negative automatic thoughts can be things such as "My boss hates me because that presentation didn't go well" or "My wife will leave me because she didn't like how I disciplined the kids." In Step 1, we discussed how to identify dysfunctional automatic thoughts. Now, we'll talk about how to challenge them. One of the most effective ways to do this is to keep a thought journal. For each entry, you'll write down three things: the situation, the emotions, and the thoughts

First, describe a situation that led to negative emotions. Recall that it can be helpful to focus on situations that lead to the most intense negative emotional outcomes. Write down what happened, where, when, and whom it was with. Then note the emotions you felt, such as anxiety, fear, or low mood, and how intensely you felt them. Finally, write down the automatic thoughts that passed through your mind during this situation. Try to identify the specific thoughts that triggered the negative feelings. To pinpoint the thoughts, you can ask yourself questions such as these: What was the worst thing I imagined during that experience? What does it mean if it's true? What does it represent? What fears or anxieties did it trigger? You can also note down how strongly you believed each thought. Try to do this exercise two to three times a day.

Once you've identified a specific negative or dysfunctional automatic thought, there are two steps to challenging it. First, look for the evidence for and against the thought. You can ask yourself questions such as these: How would someone else think about this? Is there another way of seeing this? What other possible explanations are there? Why do I think this is true? Why might this *not* be true? What would I say if someone I loved thought this about himself or herself? If I could remove the fear and anxiety, how might I see this situation? Make a list of the evidence for and against this thought. As much as you can, focus on objective, factual evidence. You may have strong beliefs or feelings related to the thought, but those are not good indicators that it is true.

For example, you might feel anxious after making a political comment to a friend who disagreed with you. One distressing thought to enter your mind might be "My friend was offended by my comment and won't want to spend time with me anymore." In writing out the evidence, you might realize your friend gave no indication they were offended. To the contrary, they said a warm good-bye and mentioned making plans for next week. In addition, you might remember a) that you have been friends for a long time, b) that you have had many other discussions on political topics before, and c) disagreeing occasionally is perfectly fine and normal. Ultimately, you will realize that the thought stems from deeper fears of losing friends and being alone. Therefore, the resulting emotions have little basis in the actual conversation.

This is a fairly minor situation, but other examples could involve events that are quite serious. Even so, automatic thoughts tend to be much more negative than necessary. Let's say you failed the final exam for a class and did not pass. The thoughts running through your mind include "I will flunk out of college!" and "I'm a failure" and "I'll never get a good job now." This is certainly unfortunate, but it's not as bad as it may seem. Upon some reflection, you might realize that the only people you know who flunked out of college failed not one but several classes. You could write down that you did pass your other three classes, that another student in the class was retaking it after failing it last semester, and that one of your professors mentioned failing a class in college.

To do this exercise, create a table with four columns: one for the thought, one for evidence for the thought, one for evidence against, and one for a new alternative thought (we'll discuss this below). You can create your own tables and include them with your other entries noting situations and emotions, or use the worksheets in the back of this book.

The next step in thought challenging is to create alternative, evidence-based thoughts. The aim is not "positive" thinking but balanced, realistic thinking. For example, if you had the thought "Everyone hates me" after overhearing a coworker tell someone that he or she didn't like you, the goal isn't to tell yourself "Everyone loves me!" Instead, imagine these two thoughts on the ends of a continuum, and find a balance between the two. Clearly, neither extreme is true. In this example, the alternative, evidence-based thought might be something like "Bill said he doesn't like me, but that doesn't mean that no one does. I have friends, family, and other coworkers who I know enjoy my company.'"

Substituting dysfunctional thoughts with positive ones is more effective than just trying to eliminate bad thoughts. People who follow a religion can challenge dysfunctional thoughts by replacing them with alternative thoughts from their tradition, such as relevant scripture. Let's take anger as an example. Perhaps you are angry after being insulted by a neighbor and have thoughts along the lines of "I have to get back at my neighbor and insult my neighbor too! I will stay angry until I get even." According to Hindu teachings, holding on to anger is like holding a hot coal and waiting to throw it at someone—it hurts the one holding it more than the one it's aimed at. When a practicing Hindu remembers this, he or she may be able to let the anger go more quickly and easily because of this imaginative framework. You can think of this as "reactivating" preexisting positive thoughts and strategies, rather than having to create completely new ones. Instead, the person could think "Being angry about my neighbor's insult hurts me more than it hurts my neighbor. I will let this go."

Similarly, Christianity and Islam both teach that success in life on earth isn't the ultimate goal—that life is more of a test and learning experience. Christians and Muslims, then, could incorporate that idea and try to see mistakes, problems, and hardships as natural and even good for their spiritual development and greater goals. Instead of thinking, "I made a mistake. I'm worthless," they could think, "I made a mistake, just as I am meant to do in my time here. How can I learn from it?"

After you've come up with an alternative thought, assess the believability of the thought. If it seems less than 50 percent believable, reexamine the evidence you listed, and try to come up with another thought that seems reasonable. You don't have to create a perfect scenario, just one that is realistic. Then, rerate your emotions associated with this scenario. Usually, you won't completely eliminate negative emotions, but you will likely be able to reduce some of the intensity.

What if your mood doesn't change at all after a few sessions of thought journaling? Sometimes, people feel little change in their emotional state after describing a situation, their emotions, and coming up with alternative thoughts. There is a series of questions you can ask yourself to improve the efficacy of the thought-journaling process. First of all, have you focused on the right situation? It's possible that the strong emotions you want to address weren't actually related to that situation, such that creating an alternative thought based on it didn't make much difference. Reassess the connection between those thoughts and the emotions you listed. You might find that there is a stronger automatic thought that is a better choice for thought journaling. If so, redo the entry with the new thought.

You may also need to come up with a new alternative thought. If your alternative thought seems unlikely or impossible, it probably won't improve your mood. Look at the evidence you listed for your chosen automatic thought, adding more if you think of any, and create a new alternative thought that seems more believable. It may also be a question of time. Devote a little more time to journaling and reflecting on your automatic thoughts. Be patient and see whether there is improvement in the next one to two weeks.

If you try some of these strategies and don't feel a difference, it could be that you still strongly believe in a dysfunctional core belief that underlies the thought. In the following step, we'll discuss how to identify and challenge dysfunctional assumptions and core beliefs.

Recap: Keeping a Thought Journal

- Identify a situation that led to anxiety or other negative emotions, and describe it in detail.
- List the emotions you experienced and their intensity (use percentages or a 1–100 scale).
- Write down the automatic thoughts that were most closely associated with the emotions and how strongly you believed these thoughts.
- Identify possible cognitive distortions in the thoughts.
- Select one or two negative thoughts and list evidence for and against them.
- Create an alternative, evidence-based thought, and rate its believability. Come up with a different thought if it seems less than 50 percent believable.
- Based on your alternative thought, rerate your original emotions, noting the emotions you feel and their intensity.
- Try the strategies listed above if you don't feel an improvement after several entries.

Dealing with Intrusive Thoughts

In Step 1, we discussed intrusive thoughts and provided examples to help you assess whether this is something you would like to work on with CBT. Now, we will go over strategies to deal with them.

Unlike automatic thoughts, intrusive thoughts are not based on dysfunctional assumptions or core beliefs—they are actually quite random. As a result, they need to be addressed in a different way than automatic thoughts. It is important not to use the same framework for intrusive thoughts as the one we just described above, since it could lead to completely incorrect conclusions about your true beliefs. There are many approaches to dealing with intrusive thoughts. Some are effective at reducing the stress associated with these thoughts, whereas others can worsen the problem. This is a good opportunity to turn to CBT techniques to constructively address the issue.

Positive Self-Talk

You can use positive self-talk to reassure yourself in the face of intrusive thoughts and diminish their power. Remind yourself that intrusive thoughts are just thoughts. They have no meaning; they don't define who you are. Even though you don't have complete control over your thoughts, you have control over your actions, and you can always decide whether you are going to do something. Remind yourself that even if you imagine doing things, it doesn't mean you actually want to or will do them. Tell yourself again what you know to be true—that you would *never* do those things. You can even use your initial distress at these thoughts to your advantage by reasoning that if they truly reflected your feelings, you wouldn't feel this upset about them.

Imagine what you would say if a loved one suffered from intrusive thoughts as well. You might reassure your loved one that he or she is a good person and that having intrusive thoughts doesn't change that. You might remind the person that intrusive thoughts are a common phenomenon, something that happens to many, many people around the world. You might say that you understand how upsetting these thoughts can be but that it's important not to take them seriously. Tell yourself all these things with the same kindness and compassion that you would show a good friend.

Acceptance

One way to deal with intrusive thoughts is acceptance. Acceptance means accepting that the thoughts happen and that you have little control over them, and refraining from trying to control them or assigning meaning to them. With time, this can decrease the power intrusive thoughts have over your emotions, and make them less distressing.

Skillful Distraction

Focusing on something engaging—something pleasant that you find totally absorbing—to take your mind off intrusive thoughts can be an effective strategy. Doing a creative hobby, such as singing, playing an instrument, or painting, being in nature, exercising, socializing, gardening, bird-watching, or reading may be helpful. Experiment with different activities, and see whether one gives you a break from intrusive thoughts. Note that skillful distraction isn't the same as trying to pretend the intrusive thoughts aren't happening. It means accepting that they are but deciding that you are not going to pay attention to them and choosing to do something fun, creative, or productive instead.

Exposure and Response Prevention

Exposure and response prevention (ERP) is the gold standard therapy for dealing with obsessive intrusive thoughts. The fundamental concept behind ERP is that when our brains encounter something on a regular basis, they learn to ignore it and treat it as meaningless. Thus, for people suffering from intrusive thoughts, intentionally creating obsessive or intrusive-type thoughts many times per day can teach their brains that these thoughts do not mean anything and can be safely disregarded.

To practice ERP, identify an intrusive thought that causes you distress. For example, if you experience violent intrusive thoughts, you could allow yourself to imagine stabbing random strangers on the street. Bring this thought to mind about ten times per day, each time realizing that you have no real desire to do such a thing. Eventually, your brain will realize that this thought is not threatening and that no emotional response is necessary. In fact, no response at all is required, and this type of thought can be easily ignored in the future.

An important thing to remember when using ERP is not to push yourself to a level that feels overwhelming. Experiencing some mild discomfort at first is normal—the idea of intentionally encouraging intrusive thoughts does sound counterintuitive—but this should subside over time as the thoughts have less and less power. Some people feel uncomfortable trying this technique on their own, and that's OK. Look for a psychologist trained in behavioral therapy (analytical therapies are not appropriate for OCD).

Spiritual Approaches

Over time, many religious and traditional belief systems have evolved ways to explain and deal with intrusive thoughts. You don't have to be religious to appreciate these ideas—often, spiritual teachings on many subjects are helpful even if we don't practice the faith as a whole. This can be true even when we find religious explanations illogical or farfetched. The brilliance of many religions is that they provide a meaningful narrative about the human experience, and you are free to co-opt whatever you like and reject whatever you don't.

One of the most reassuring explanations of intrusive thoughts comes from Islam, which clearly identifies them as originating *outside* the individual. Islam teaches that the human heart is naturally pure and good but that the mind can be affected by *Waswas*—evil whispers from the devil. The devil is clever and tries to make us think that these are our own thoughts, so that we doubt our intentions and desires. But being aware of this allows people who follow Islam to easily dismiss upsetting or "bad" thoughts as external and not reflective of the true nature of their hearts, thus greatly diminishing the distress and shame associated with intrusive thoughts. Whether people believe this literally or metaphorically, it offers a framework for dealing with intrusive thoughts, and relief from needless stress.

Medication

Finally, some people may find medication effective in reducing the frequency of intrusive thoughts. One example is Maria Bamford, a stand-up comedian who has struggled with obsessive-compulsive disorder, bipolar disorder, anxiety, and suicidal thoughts since adolescence. She has bravely shared her story through her comedy and interviews with journalists and radio hosts in an effort to destigmatize mental illness. On an episode of the APM podcast *The Hilarious World of Depression*, she described how she experienced terribly upsetting intrusive thoughts, including worries that she might kill her own family or sexually molest animals. After beginning medication, she noticed a vast improvement in the frequency of her intrusive thoughts.

Since medications can have serious side effects, it's best to try talk therapy or self-directed CBT first. But medications can provide profound relief from intrusive thoughts, so don't hesitate to discuss the possibility with a doctor or psychiatrist.

It's important to remember that some maladaptive strategies may seem to work in the short term but can make intrusive thoughts worse over time. One of these is *avoidance.* Some people find that certain situations trigger intrusive thoughts, and attempt to solve the problem by avoiding those situations. However, this creates anxiety around such situations, which can become extremely limiting and disruptive to normal life, reinforcing the belief that the intrusive thoughts are true.

Another generally ineffective strategy is attempting to control these thoughts. People who have upsetting intrusive thoughts may try to force their minds to stop thinking those things. This usually does not work, as trying hard not to think of something tends to make us focus on it even more! Thus, attempts at control can cause greater distress when you realize that you cannot control your intrusive thoughts. As we said above, it is better to accept right away that you do not control them, and then work on other strategies to reduce the frequency and distress associated with them

Step 5: Identifying Assumptions and Core Beliefs

If you have identified dysfunctional automatic thoughts as a problem you want to address, and have completed the exercises in the previous steps, use Step 5 to challenge these thinking styles on a deeper level. Remember that this is not the same approach as challenging intrusive thoughts. Do not apply the framework for dysfunctional assumptions and core beliefs to intrusive thoughts.

Identifying Dysfunctional Assumptions

Intermediate beliefs are collections of assumptions, conditional rules, and attitudes that arise from core beliefs and heavily influence automatic thoughts. They often center on achievement, acceptance, and control and may be expressed in an *if-then* form—for example, "If I made more money, then my family would love me more" and "If you offend people, they will reject you." They can also be *should* or *must* statements, such as "I should get straight As" and "I should never ask for help." The problem is that these assumptions, rules, and attitudes are often rigid and unrealistic. They include high standards but fail to account for the unexpected life events that may make it hard or impossible to meet those standards. They reinforce dysfunctional core beliefs and increase the mental bias that leads to negative automatic thoughts as we take in information.

Once you've spent some time noticing your automatic thoughts, you can try to identify the assumptions that underlie them. Look at your list of automatic thoughts, and see whether any themes or underlying ideas, rules, or attitudes stand out. Sometimes, your automatic thoughts directly express dysfunctional assumptions. Look at your list again, and see whether there are any *if-then* or *should* statements or ideas that communicate an assumption or belief about the world.

You can also spend some time thinking about your beliefs in relation to the problem. For example, if you have a lot of anxiety around your job, you might come up with a set of assumptions including "If my boss perceives me as incompetent, then I will lose my job" or "If I don't do well on this project, I will appear incompetent" or "If I lose this job, I'll never find another good one." These are assumptions and attitudes that support a certain type of automatic thought that leads to your anxiety about work.

Identifying Dysfunctional Core Beliefs

Underlying intermediate beliefs and assumptions is another, deeper layer known as core beliefs. They are generalized, inflexible, absolute, basic beliefs that people hold about themselves, others, and the world. They are broader than assumptions and affect all areas of life. Rather than being just reactions to situations, core beliefs shape how we understand what we see, thus shaping our assumptions, thoughts, and emotions. They can be positive and helpful, or dysfunctional.

Core beliefs are often formed in childhood and reinforced throughout life. They can also form during traumatic events in adulthood, such as the death of a loved one, fighting in a war, or being the victim of a violent crime. We tend to accept evidence that supports our beliefs and reject evidence that does not, so we may hold our core beliefs strongly even if there is little evidence for them. We often support dysfunctional core beliefs by focusing on one or two areas of our lives that aren't going well, rather than looking at our lives overall. However, with cognitive behavioural therapy, you can challenge and change dysfunctional core beliefs. It's important to remember that core beliefs are *ideas*, not facts. How strongly you feel something is not an indicator of how true it is.

Here are some common dysfunctional core beliefs:

- I am incompetent.
- I am unlovable.
- I am a failure.
- I am worthless.
- I am trapped.
- I cannot cope with grief or loss.
- I will never be happy.
- Happiness requires perfection.
- Happiness requires success.
- The world is cruel.
- There's no point to anything.
- Others cannot be trusted.
- The world is mostly bad.

To identify core beliefs, you will have to do some digging within yourself. Some people have a hard time understanding how their thought processes connect to negative emotions, so it may be helpful to start by identifying automatic thoughts and assumptions before core beliefs. Some people may also find it painful to explore their core beliefs, so it may be better to start by addressing automatic thoughts.

Once you are ready to examine your core beliefs, it can be helpful to look at lists of automatic thoughts and assumptions that you have identified. Look for themes across them. Is there something unsaid or assumed that you believe is true about all these statements, a foundation on which they all rest? For example, someone might have a set of assumptions that includes the statements "If I do well in school, my parents will love me" and "If I work out more, my peers will love me." A possible core belief leading to both of these intermediate beliefs is "I am not loved" or "I am unlovable." Also, you could discover that you hold a core belief along the lines of "People are mostly bad" if your automatic thoughts consistently reflect assumptions that people have bad intentions.

Think about things that seem too obvious to say, and then say them. We are often so sure of our core beliefs that we think they don't merit examination. You can ask yourself other questions to help elicit your core beliefs: What is the world like? What am I like? What are others like? What is the future like? Is there meaning? Do I view myself as a valued member of the community? Am I lovable? Am I hopeful? Can I deal with difficult situations?

Another useful technique that therapists use is called the downward-arrow technique. Beginning with a distressing automatic thought, ask yourself, "What does this mean?" For each answer, ask the question repeatedly until you arrive at a fundamental, core belief that has no deeper meaning. For example, someone could be depressed after becoming paralyzed in a car accident. Asking "What does that mean?" might result in the following responses: I am paralyzed → I can't take care of myself → Someone has to take care of me → I am a burden to society → I have no value. In this way, the person identifies the dysfunctional core belief "I have no value." Once core beliefs are identified, you can challenge them and try to create healthier beliefs.

Challenging Dysfunctional Assumptions and Beliefs

Core beliefs can be much harder to challenge than automatic thoughts, because they are deeply ingrained. We may not even know what our core beliefs are, until we spend time actively trying to understand them. This is an important long-term step in CBT because if you challenge automatic thoughts without challenging the underlying beliefs, the same or other dysfunctional automatic thoughts may return again and again.

To challenge core beliefs, you can use a method

similar to the thought journal. Keep a list of assumptions and core beliefs that you have identified using the methods suggested above. You can ask friends, family, or experts on a certain subject for their thoughts on the truthfulness of these ideas. Write down evidence to support the assumption or belief and evidence that conflicts with it, and decide whether it is reasonable. You can also ask yourself questions about these assumptions, such as the following:

- Is this a reasonable expectation?
- Does this account for human fallibility?
- Is this a helpful assumption?
- Does everyone hold himself or herself to this standard?
- Is this really true? Is this true for everyone?
- Would I tell that to the people I love?
- What makes me think I have to do that?
- Can I reject that idea?
- What examples have I seen where that didn't appear to be true?

One way to challenge core beliefs is to create a chart describing multiple areas of your life that you view as important and that relate to your core belief. Often, people base core beliefs such as "I'm a failure" on just one or two areas of their lives, so making this chart can provide a more balanced picture. You can make a pie chart that shows how important each aspect is, or simply write a list. Let's say you have a core belief of "I am a failure." You might write down *having a good job*, *having a stable relationship*, *having children*, *having a home*, and *being respected in the community* as parts of life that contribute to feeling like a success or a failure. Then, assess how you're doing in each area. After doing this, you can realize that despite troubles at work, you feel authentically successful in other parts of life. By remembering this, you will adjust your core beliefs within a few weeks.

It's also possible while doing this activity to conclude, for example, that a marriage really is heading toward failure. However, you can separate that from the core belief of *being* a failure by remembering that you're a valued parent and community member, and use this as an opportunity to face challenges in the marriage.

"Behavioral experiments" can be another powerful strategy to emotionally challenge resistant core beliefs that remain in place even when you have "intellectually" challenged them. To do this, contrast your dysfunctional core belief with one you would prefer to hold. For example, replace "People are mostly bad" with "People are mostly good." Make specific predictions about what will happen if this is true. Then, go about daily activities, and keep a log of evidence to support this belief. Viewing it as an experiment may help you suspend your contrary emotional belief so you can consider the evidence in a more balanced way. Hopefully, this experiment will help demonstrate that a dysfunctional core belief is not true. But it's possible for your experiences to reinforce dysfunctional core beliefs that are actually false, so this method may be best used with a therapist.

Using Philosophy and Spirituality to Change Dysfunctional Core Beliefs

At an individual level, some core beliefs arise from personal circumstances and experiences. In other cases, cultures, especially Western consumer culture, reinforce dysfunctional core beliefs related to success, happiness, love, perfection, and fulfillment. It may feel difficult to convince yourself that these messages are false, because we are constantly bombarded with them. Rather than simply providing a single alternative belief, spiritual and philosophical traditions can provide a complete alternative narrative that allows you to challenge dysfunctional beliefs in a more holistic way.

In ancient times, there were no psychologists or therapists, but philosophy and religion offered relief from anxiety, depression, grief, and other troubles, and ancient spiritual traditions often incorporated mental health practices into religious beliefs and rituals. Tools like prayer and meditation were designed to soothe the mind, relieve stress, and make a person more effective at dealing with challenges.

Philosophy and spirituality can provide many benefits today, too. People who practice a religion may find it helpful to combine faith with CBT, but holy texts offer plenty of wisdom that anyone can appreciate, as well as messages about hope and perseverance through difficult periods, and a broader perspective on life. Those who prefer to avoid spiritual approaches can gain much wisdom from philosophy. Seek out philosophers or people of faith in your community who can offer respectful, nonjudgmental wisdom and advice.

In fact, spirituality is increasingly being integrated into CBT, especially for treating patients with lasting depression. Religiously integrated cognitive behavioral therapy (RCBT) combines patients' spiritual beliefs with CBT and helps them develop positive alternative thoughts and helpful actions through their own accepted faith-based beliefs, practices, and resources. Behavioral therapists have come up with treatment approaches for five of the major religions in the world—Buddhism, Hinduism, Islam, Judaism, and Christianity.

Meditation and prayer, proven to reduce stress and lessen the severity of depression, are aspects of spiritual traditions that are often incorporated into RCBT. Reading scripture that relates to a patient's situation might also be included. For example, a Hindu patient might meditate on this verse from the Bhagavad Gita: "The man of steady wisdom, having subdued them all (senses), becomes fixed in Me, The Supreme. His wisdom is well established whose senses are under control." Likewise, patients who follow Buddhist teachings can benefit from this passage from the Dhammapada: "Meditation brings wisdom; lack of meditation leaves ignorance. Know well what leads you forward and what holds you back, and choose the path that leads to wisdom."

Patients are also encouraged to engage with other members of their faith and use spiritual resources. Group activities, including worship, religious services, charity activities, meditation retreats in Buddhism, *swadhyaya* in

Hinduism, and activities in mosques, help to bring about a sense of purpose. This builds a sense of empathy for others and moves the focus away from the self.

Sometimes, the value systems promoted by spiritual traditions clash with those promoted by contemporary CBT researchers and practitioners. In some cases, organized religions actively promote dysfunctional core beliefs, or rituals that cause suffering and harm. It is important to follow your faith if you profoundly believe it to be true, helpful, and good, even if it's not popular. However, if you realize that a religious belief you hold is damaging to you or others, this is a good opportunity to reexamine it and seek alternative understandings. In every faith, scholars have been debating meanings and interpretations for hundreds—or thousands!—of years, and you have every right to do this as well. The concept of sin in particular causes distress to many people. We will present an alternative view of sin after exploring several faiths that can support you through the CBT process.

Eastern Philosophy and CBT

Taoism

Taoism offers helpful alternative beliefs that can complement CBT, especially the concept of wu wei. Taoism (or Daoism) is an ancient Chinese philosophy or way of life based on the writings of Lao Tzu. It promotes unity with nature, pursuit of spiritual development, and leading a virtuous life. Taoism emphasizes searching for a way of living that feels easy and natural and avoiding unnecessary struggle and suffering.

Sometime around the fifth century BC, Lao Tzu or someone writing under his name wrote down many of his philosophical ideas about the universe and the keys to a happy, moral life. The book, titled *Tao Te Ching*, is the basis for Taoism. Lao Tzu held certain spiritual beliefs about the universe, and today many people worship deities associated with Taoism in temples. This is religious Taoism. However, Lao Tzu's ideas are also followed by many as a philosophy. Philosophical Taoism is compatible with religions and secular humanism and can offer guidance and wisdom alongside other traditions. It is similar to Buddhism in this kind of flexibility and openness to many belief systems.

The most important concept in Taoism is that of tao,

which means "the way" or "the path." Tao is not a deity and is not worshipped; rather, it is representative of the correct way of doing things and of the life-force or energy of the universe. Practitioners of Taoism often think of themselves as following or being on the tao.

Much of Taoism revolves around the concept of wu wei, which roughly translates to "doing by not doing" or "doing without trying." It can also be thought of as doing things effortlessly, following the path of least resistance. Lao Tzu believed that people should search for the simple, natural way of doing things rather than making them hard and complicated. The general attitude is one of acceptance and nonstruggle. This can be helpful in countering the Western idea that we should always be struggling and working hard, if for no other reason than the sake of work itself.

Many of Lao Tzu's writings in the *Tao Te Ching* express this idea of wu wei. He wrote, "The sage acts by doing nothing" (chapter 2). He believed that this helped avoid conflict and ensured a peaceful existence, explaining that "because [the sage] opposes no one, no one in the world can oppose him" (chapter 22).

Practicing wu wei doesn't mean that we abandon everything or stop caring whether certain things happen; it means that we take a radically different approach to achieving those goals. As Lao Tzu says, "The Way is ever without action, yet nothing is left undone" (chapter 37). In fact, trying to do everything can result in little being achieved: "The highest virtue does nothing. Yet, nothing needs to be done. The lowest virtue does everything. Yet, much remains to be done" (chapter 38).

You may be able to apply the concept of wu wei in your own life, especially in situations where little productive action can be taken but many strong emotions are swirling around, creating a strong desire to act. A good example is seeking happiness. It's something we all hope for, and we sometimes go to extreme lengths to get or achieve the things we think will make us happy. The ironic reality is that these things—wealth, success, beauty, fame, popularity—often don't make us nearly as happy as we expected. You may find that abandoning a conscious struggle to be happy and focusing instead on finding meaning and acceptance makes you happier, without directly trying.

Similarly, being in a romantic relationship that seems to be failing makes most people panic, and they try extremely hard to fix it and make it work. Sometimes it does, but their actions can also make it worse, prolong relationships that are going to end anyway, and hide deeper problems. A wu wei approach might be to stop conscious efforts to fix the relationship, and focus on *being*: being kind, honest, compassionate, and accepting. Search for open communication and sincere connection, and you will likely see the nature of the relationship, and its future, more clearly than if you remain focused on fixing it.

Wu wei can work for dealing with anxiety too. Often, we try to take on anxiety directly by reasoning with anxious thoughts or trying to stop them. Telling ourselves to calm down often backfires, and we end up even more nervous! Lao Tzu might have seen this as going against the flow, trying to push energy in the opposite direction. Instead, try a technique known as *anxious reappraisal*, which essentially means reidentifying your anxious energy as excitement. Anxiety and excitement are similar physiologically—both involve increased heart rate and breathing, higher levels of certain hormones, and sweating or shaking. But where anxiety is associated with a threat, excitement is associated with opportunity and intense positive emotions. Next time you start to feel anxious, tell yourself repeatedly that you are excited, revved up, or super motivated. With this technique you simply redirect the flow of energy rather than trying to stop or reverse it, which is much harder.

If you liked this concept of doing by not doing, you can learn more about Taoism by reading the *Tao Te Ching*, the collected writings of Lao Tzu. It is available free online.

Hinduism

A particularly meaningful time in which spirituality can play a role in the CBT process is when a death occurs. Losing a loved one is a painful aspect of our impermanent lives here, and it prompts many people to seek solace and wisdom from faith. Spiritual traditions have ways of explaining and dealing with death that make it more bearable for the living.

In Hindu tradition, the soul is immortal, merely dwelling in the body for a time before moving on: "It cannot be pierced, nor burned, nor wet, nor dried. It is eternal, all-pervading, unchangeable, immovable, everlasting." Then, explains the Bhagavad Gita, an important Hindu scripture, "As man casts off worn-out garments and puts on others which are new, similarly the embodied soul, casting off worn-out bodies, enters into others which are new...This (Self, or soul) is said to be unmanifested, unthinkable, unchangeable; therefore knowing this to be so, thou shouldst not grieve...The dweller in the body of everyone is ever indestructible; therefore...thou shouldst not grieve over any creature." For some, the idea that the soul of a loved one is not gone but eternally moving though time, like their own, can be comforting.

Buddhism

Buddhist teachings are perhaps the most similar to concepts in CBT, and they continue to influence its development. Interestingly, Dr. Beck, the cofounder of CBT, practices Buddhist mindfulness meditation, and the Dalai Lama has followed the development of CBT, noting its similarities to Buddhism in the process of watching thoughts, separating them from reality, and examining alternative ways of thinking. Many people suffering from anxiety, depression, and other mental health conditions have found some solace in Buddhism.

Buddhism teaches practitioners techniques to keep the mind calm, view themselves as part of a larger whole, observe thoughts and feeling without becoming overwhelmed by them, and treat everyone, including themselves, with kindness and compassion. Many Buddhists work toward cultivating a sense of profound peace through a regular meditation practice.

Some Buddhist teachings can seem strange at first but ultimately provide relief from anxiety and depression. Buddhism says that the self is an illusion, a realization arrived at through meditation. What we think of as the self is a collection of a physical body, beliefs, thoughts, feelings, and sensations; thus, we literally make ourselves with our thoughts, as the quotation at the beginning of the book says. However, our strong belief in the existence of a self can be problematic when the concepts we use to define ourselves change or are destructive. We are so insistent on the notion of self that the thought of its destruction is extremely upsetting. Accordingly, Buddhism also emphasizes the impermanent nature of life and teaches followers to learn to live with uncertainty. We tend to want to believe that something about us and our world is permanent, yet everything, from empires to anthills, is in a state of constant flux. Clinging to the belief that things are permanent leads to distress when they do inevitably change.

If you haven't encountered these beliefs before, they could easily be upsetting. The idea that there is no self seems absurd! With time, however, Buddhist teachings could allow you to discard many of the dysfunctional assumptions and beliefs you hold about what you should do and how others see you, and teach you how to live with kindness and compassion in the face of uncertainty.

Islam

Islam is an Abrahamic faith practiced by approximately 1.6 billion people around the world. The most essential beliefs are the existence of one God who created the universe, the earth, and humans and, out of his love for them, sent a series of prophets with guidance and instructions. The last of these prophets is Mohammed, who received the Qur'an in the seventh century. Islam teaches that the world is temporary and that a person's true life is the one that comes after, in which anyone who chooses goodness over evil and seeks God can return to dwell in total peace with him. Thus, this life is a sort of test for people, who have been given complete free will by God.

Many scholars hold an inclusive view of what being Muslim means. If someone hears of the Prophet Mohammed and the message he brought and believes that it is true, he or she would be expected to accept the faith. However, someone who had never heard of this or didn't have a chance to understand it would also be considered a Muslim just by his or her belief in one God (or a Great Spirit, or simply a belief in the goodness of the human heart) and the oneness of creation and his or her commitment to searching for truth, doing good, and abstaining from evil. Similarly, many understand the verses in the Qur'an that mention "disbelievers" to be referring to those who are willfully ignorant, reject truth and goodness outright, or actively attack Muslims for their beliefs, not to peaceful people who just don't happen to be practicing Muslims.

Thus, you don't have to have been raised Muslim to appreciate the lessons of kindness, community, charity, and forgiveness that the Qur'an teaches or to take comfort in its reassurance of mercy and ultimate peace.

Many Muslims find their faith profoundly reassuring in the face of difficulties, anxiety, and grief, because the resounding message is that no matter how hard it is in this life, if you do your best to be a good person and search for closeness with the divine, everything will be OK in the end. Ultimately, there is an end to suffering through the mercy of God.

Many verses in the Qur'an repeat the phrase "no fear shall be upon them, nor shall they grieve":

> Those who believe (in the Qur'an), and those who follow the Jewish (scriptures), and the Christians and the Sabians, any who believe in Allah and the Last Day, and work righteousness, shall have their reward with their Lord; on them shall be no fear, nor shall they grieve. (2:62)

> Those who (in charity) spend of their goods by night and by day, in secret and in public, have their reward with their Lord: on them shall be no fear, nor shall they grieve. (2:274)

> Behold! Verily on the friends of Allah there is no fear,

nor shall they grieve. (10:62)

This is deeply meaningful because fear and grief are two of the most difficult aspects of the human experience, and Islam teaches that anyone who seeks truth and goodness can be free of these things forever. (The verses above are from the Yusuf Ali translation.) Other aspects of the faith may be helpful too: daily rituals of calming prayer, a reverence for the natural world, an emphasis on family and social ties, a sense of community, a call to think beyond yourself to those most in need, and the knowledge that one can always call on a higher power for strength and support. Islam, like many religions, depends on the practitioner's reasonable and kindhearted interpretation of the text.

One of the thinkers who best capture the philosophical and mystical aspects of Islam—perhaps of humanity as a whole—is Rumi, a thirteenth-century Persian Sufi poet. His elegant and succinct verses speak to timeless aspects of the human condition: love, hope, hardship, good and evil, loneliness, pain, and joy. Recurrent themes are loving and living to the fullest, accepting pain and hardship as part of the learning experience that is life, seeking the divine, and being a good person. Some of his writings describe the most mundane aspects of life; others, the most transcendent moments. His understanding of spirituality is broad, and his poems show that he believed in many paths to truth. For him, this truth took the form of a loving, merciful, and mysterious deity, from which we came and to which we will return.

Rumi was a prolific writer, and guidance, wisdom, and reassurance for almost any problem can be found somewhere in his works. Many of his thousands of verses are available for free online or collected into anthologies arranged by topic. Below are a few selected verses that touch on subjects relevant to this book. Give them some thought, and look for more of Rumi's poetry if you enjoy them.

> Your task is not to seek for love, but merely to seek and find all the barriers within yourself that you have built against it.

> Before death takes away what you are given, give away what there is to give.

> Out beyond ideas of wrongdoing and rightdoing there is a field. / I'll meet you there. / When the soul lies down in that grass the world is too full to talk about.

> The wound is the place where light enters you.

Yesterday I was clever, so I wanted to change the world. Today I am wise, so I am changing myself.

Be empty of worrying. Think of who created thought! / Why do you stay in prison / When the door is so wide open?

Sorrow prepares you for joy. It violently sweeps everything out of your house, so that new joy can find space to enter. It shakes the yellow leaves from the bough of your heart, so that fresh, green leaves can grow in their place. It pulls up the rotten roots, so that new roots hidden beneath have room to grow. Whatever sorrow shakes from your heart, far better things will take their place.

This being human is a guest house. Every morning is a new arrival. A joy, a depression, a meanness, some momentary awareness comes as an unexpected visitor...Welcome and entertain them all. Treat each guest honorably. The dark thought, the shame, the malice, meet them at the door laughing, and invite them in. Be grateful for whoever comes, because each has been sent as a guide from beyond.

Christian, Jew, Muslim, shaman, Zoroastrian, stone, ground, mountain, river, each has a secret way of being with the mystery, unique and not to be judged.

Be a lamp, or a lifeboat, or a ladder. Help someone's soul heal. Walk out of your house like a shepherd.

When you feel a peaceful joy, that's when you are near truth.

A Different Way of Understanding Sin

Many people shy away from discussions of sin—understandably. In Western culture, sin has become associated primarily with guilt, damnation, and moralizing by closed-minded individuals with questionable motivations. Sin has been used as a political tool—a way to condemn minorities, define outgroups, and grant more power to religious authorities. Often, it has promoted discord, misery, and violence. When the concept is abused in this way, little is achieved in the way of making people kinder, better, or more merciful, and often much harm is done. People are made to feel guilty without an offer of hope or an accessible approach to mending harmful ways. Where did this come from?

In the mid-three hundreds in North Africa, a devout Christian named Augustine came up with a novel idea: original sin. Augustine, who would be canonized by Pope Boniface VIII around 1300, argued that all humans bore the stain of Adam's first transgression in the Garden of Eden and were hopelessly corrupt, depending completely on God's grace for salvation. Neither the Bible nor Jesus described such a concept, and it was hotly debated at the time. Despite the controversy, it was adopted by the ancient Roman Catholic Church and has had profound impacts on Western thought until the present day. Even as Europeans and Americans become less and less religious and science takes primacy in explaining the universe, this idea continues to affect how we see ourselves. One and a half millennia after Augustine, many Westerners subconsciously see themselves as inherently flawed or bad, a notion that baffles people in many Eastern and indigenous societies.

We don't have to see it this way.

In order to dissuade ourselves of this sense that no

matter what we *do*, we *are* bad, we can learn to understand ancient religious and spiritual teachings about sin in a new way. Rather than as accusation or condemnation, they can be seen as a chance to shift our direction from a path of fear and destruction to a path of love and healing.

As we begin this discussion, remind yourself that *you* are not bad. You are good; you are whole; you are worthy of love. You can *have* thoughts or patterns of thinking that are harmful, and you can *do* actions that are harmful to yourself and others. But these things are not who you are; they are choices. And where there are choices, you can always choose a path of love and healing. For you, this path may lead to a sense of closeness with a deity, to reconciliation with family or a community, or simply to greater peace within yourself.

What Do World Religions Identify as Cardinal Sins or Vices?

You don't have to subscribe to any religious beliefs in order to benefit from the ancient wisdom that the Torah, the Bible, the Qur'an, Buddhist, Sikh or Hindu scriptures offer about avoiding styles of thought and emotion that predictably cause great pain.

If we look at what different faiths define as major sins or vices to be avoided, we find a stunning continuity across continents and millennia. Catholicism teaches that there are seven cardinal sins from which all other sins follow: lust, greed, anger, envy, pride, sloth, and gluttony. Ancient Sikh scriptures teach that the "five thieves who live within this body are lust, anger, greed, attachment and ego. They rob us of ambrosia, but the egocentrics do not understand it and no one listens to their cries" (Guru Amar Das, Sorath). Some schools of Buddhism identify five poisons that pollute our souls and actions. They roughly translate as desire and attachment to the world, anger or hatred, jealousy and envy, ignorance, and pride or arrogance. Similarly, Islam condemns pride and arrogance, lust, greed, overindulgence, anger, and cruelty or a lack of mercy.

The same themes show up again and again in religions from around the world, throughout millennia of human history: Don't be jealous of what others have, but accept your life and circumstances. Enjoy life, but don't get overly attached to this world or its pleasures, or to your worldly possessions and achievements. Don't be prideful or think that you are better than or fit to judge others. Don't let your desire control you, whether it is for money, power, or sex. Don't let your anger get out of control, and be merciful toward those who have wronged you. Seek understanding and accept truth wherever you find it; don't remain in ignorance.

Most religions also describe specific actions that are unlawful, again with striking similarity across different faiths. Nearly all prohibit killing aside from self-defense, theft, dishonesty, sex outside of a sincere and acknowledged relationship ("marriage" isn't always a useful word since its definition has varied over time and across cultures), and loss of control through drugs or alcohol.

In opposition to the sins or vices that lead to bad and harmful actions, religions emphasize qualities that encourage good actions that relieve the suffering of one's self and others: humility, patience, kindness, generosity, temperance, acceptance (of inevitable hardships, not of injustice), mercy, transcendence of worldly concerns, and pursuit of knowledge and truth. Many require or recommend similar benevolent actions too: respect for parents and elders, giving in charity, reverence for life, some sort of ritual prayer or meditation, and a search for spiritual knowledge.

If such similar commandments have been taught by such diverse faiths across time and space, they are worth serious consideration as advice on life, whether you view this as divine revelation or simply wise guidance stemming from a deep understanding of the basic goodness of human nature.

Why Are These Things Sins?

Sins aren't sins because God (or prophets or a divine spirit or some particularly wise ancient writers—however you choose to interpret sacred texts) wanted to make our lives harder or less fun or just make us feel bad. They are sins because they bring mental and emotional suffering to the self and others. Often, they separate us from others and lead to isolation and loneliness—unnatural, painful states for human beings. We long for connection and belonging, but actions that are profoundly self-centered and harmful to others make this impossible.

Think of greed, for example. Countless horrible things have been done because a few people wanted more for themselves. Greed has led to theft, murder, and environmental destruction, actions that cause great harm to other people. In addition, greed makes people deeply unsatisfied with their own lives. Though they may have plenty, they will never feel that what they have is sufficient, and they will be trapped in endless suffering.

Similarly, an inflated ego prevents us from being truly good. Hinduism teaches that ego is at the root of all evil. Letting go of ego leads to greater acceptance, forgiveness, gratitude, and reduced emotional stress. In the Hindu (as well as Buddhist) tradition, such a state is conducive to attaining nirvana, the ultimate bliss. Hinduism urges followers to avoid sins not to make life harder but to have a better chance of attaining nirvana!

Or consider desire. In the context of a consensual, respectful relationship, sex can be harmless as well as a source of joy and pleasure. Certainly, sex and sexual desire are normal and wonderful parts of the human experience. Why, then, would lust or desire be considered a sin? It is because when desire is given free rein, when it becomes the focus, it tends to be destructive.

One way of understanding this is that when pleasure becomes completely uncoupled from meaning, it tends to lead to suffering one way or another. For example, when sex becomes completely disconnected from an emotional or intellectual relationship with another person, it is more likely to become exploitative, risky, and physically or emotionally harmful. In addition, people who are suffering intensely sometimes seek pleasure—through sex, alcohol, drugs, or other means—as a way to deal with the pain. This isn't a question of people being bad; it's a situation in which they need help to address pain in more constructive ways. It makes sense, however, why this use of pleasure would still be considered a "sin": it puts you in danger, delays true alleviation of suffering, and often hurts the people that you love the most. This is not an issue of moralizing anyone's choices; rather, it is about how a desire for pleasure before a desire for connection can cause suffering.

Avoiding Sin

How then can we avoid sins, the actions and styles of thinking that bring us and others pain and isolation? One of the most powerful ways to do this is to create positive meaning and connection. We need meaning and connection, and we will find a way to get them, whether good or bad. For example, for some gang members, their membership in a violent gang provides connection and a sense of purpose and identity. It's wrong but understandable. For someone else, an all-consuming obsession with accumulating money and material wealth may create a sense of meaning, at the expense of time spent with loved ones and of ethical principles.

Finding positive opportunities for connection and meaning is much better. Build and repair relationships with loved ones and new friends. Care for animals, children, the sick, or the elderly. Find a cause. Volunteer for an organization. Join a club. There is always, always someone in need of help, and being the person to provide it can help you just as much. While it's important to directly address "sins" as well, strengthening these other things in our lives can make it much easier. You might be surprised at how, in a connected and meaningful life, jealously, greed, empty desire, anger, and pride can fade on their own.

Take a moment now to remind yourself that you are not inherently bad or sinful. Sins are a way of thinking about actions and thinking styles that could be causing you to suffer more or causing suffering for those you love. It doesn't mean that you are bad, evil, beyond redemption, or condemned, just that you could make some changes to allow you to live better and more peacefully.

Stoicism and CBT

Stoicism, a philosophy stretching back to ancient Greece, is a source of meaningful wisdom that has inspired many concepts in CBT. Epictetus, a first-century Stoic philosopher, wrote that "man is disturbed not by things, but by the views he takes of them." Two thousand years later, this became the central idea of cognitive therapy. In the words of Dr. Albert Ellis, "People don't just get upset. They contribute to their upsetness." The answer then, according to Epictetus, is "to make the best of what is in our power, and take the rest as it naturally happens."

Stoicism is an "operating system" for leading a better

life. Stoicism holds that a virtuous life is a good life, and offers principles of virtuous behavior based on generations of observation and trial and error. Stoicism is also about accepting fate, reality, or the "laws of the universe," including factors beyond the perceptions of our minds. Stoicism asserts that reason is our human connection to these laws. Therefore, we must use reason independently of likes and dislikes, pain and pleasure, and everyday desires and worries.

Stoicism encourages rational thinking, self-awareness, and practical wisdom and teaches that we should avoid being overly attached to certain outcomes or desires. It teaches us to be aware of our stream-of-consciousness thoughts and to be slow to accept and emotionally react to them. As with CBT, the idea is that unchecked automatic thoughts can cause negative emotions, so we should carefully examine thoughts before reacting emotionally. The general strategy of ancient Stoicism is, once a thought has been identified, to evaluate whether it relates to something that is under your control. If not, the thought should be let go.

Stoics believe that tranquility can be achieved by developing a clear understanding of what is under our control (our minds) and what is not (everything else), and then fully accepting that reality and what results from it. A

Latin phrase, *amor fati* (a love of fate), became popular among Stoic practitioners, who reasoned that what must be accepted may as well be embraced lovingly. They argued that confusion about what we have influence over is a cause of suffering. Just as fish have minimal influence in the ocean, we humans have only minimal influence in the universe. This is not to say we have no power; rather, we should focus our efforts inward, toward our own minds and attitudes. Not doing so leads to pointless struggle and suffering.

CBT borrows from Stoicism in three fundamental areas: logic, acceptance, and right action. Let's look at these in more detail.

Logic, according to Stoics, is the filter that separates the wise from the unwise. We often see things as we imagine them to be rather than how they really are. The truth becomes distorted by dysfunctional cognitive frameworks, resulting in destructive emotions and suffering. This gap between perception and reality can be distinguished only by logic. Logic dictates that rather than attempting to change nature, you need to change your thoughts to align with reality. The more you're successful at doing this, the more you'll be able to fill the gaps, and the less you'll suffer.

Accepting nature—with all its ups and downs and

good and bad—is the second key tenet of Stoicism. This reflects a duality taught by many religions: For every light, there's darkness; for every pleasure, there's pain. Suffering, agony, and death are as much part of the natural law as happiness, pleasure, and birth, all occurring in turn. There's beauty in this world, and there's terror too. Accept both for a balanced, contented life.

This does not mean that Stoicism enables passivity and fatalism. Stoicism encourages right action—the third tenet—when possible and accepts inaction only when the outcomes are not within human control. This concept is echoed in the famous Serenity Prayer written by American theologian Reinhold Niebuhr:

Grant me the **serenity**
To *accept* the things I cannot change,
Courage to change the things I *can*,
And the **wisdom** to know the *difference*.

The third tenet of right action is based on the teaching that we cannot change what happens to us but we can change how we respond. If someone insults us in public, there's nothing we can do to change that fact after it has occurred, but we can control how we react. Stoics believe that rather than waste energy on trying to control external circumstances, we should spend that same energy on controlling our responses to those circumstances in a positive way. This eventually helps to change the world—one individual at a time—and even could assist in controlling the circumstances that caused this change in the first place. Stoicism also encourages taking actions that promote well-being and avoiding those that harm it.

Negative Visualization

One particular Stoic technique that fits well with CBT is negative visualization. Negative visualization is based on the idea that imagining possible or inevitable negative events ahead of time prepares us for their possible occurrence. As a result, they will be less shocking, and we will be better equipped to either prevent them or deal with them. Negative visualization can help address some types of intrusive thoughts, especially worry intrusions.

Negative visualization dates back to the Roman Stoic philosophers Seneca and Epictetus. Before taking a trip, for example, Seneca would imagine everything that could possibly go wrong, and adjust his plans so he could avoid or deal with the bad possibilities. Think of this part as a practical exercise: in the situation that is causing you stress or generating intrusive worry thoughts, logically go through the series of events and assess where problems could occur. In some cases, you may realize that things you are worried about are extremely unlikely to occur, or downright impossible. That can help put your mind at ease. For other possibilities, make a plan. Taking preventive action can help address unproductive anxiety.

Negative visualization can also be used to help us value what we have, by imagining our lives without it. This can be useful even when we are unlikely to lose something. For example, married couples might grow accustomed to each other over time, some to the point that they forget how important they are to each other and take the other's presence for granted. This could lead one or both of them to treat the other with indifference or contempt, to ignore each other, or even to do things that are incredibly hurtful, like beginning an affair with a new partner.

Stoic philosophers believe that this attitude can be prevented by frequently imagining life without one's spouse. Even though it can feel upsetting, a husband or wife who imagines life without the other each morning is likely to be more appreciative, grateful, and loving. It can prompt them to make better use of the time they have together, such that they are less likely to separate and that when one does die, the other can grieve without feeling regret.

You can try it with anything in your life that you want to value more—a parent, partner, or child; your health, your home, or your ability to work; or living in a safe neighborhood or a country with political freedoms. Imagine in detail your life without that thing. Would it be harder? Less joyful? More lonely? Less meaningful? Thing about it; then be sure to translate that newfound appreciation into action. Tell your loved ones how important they are to you. Be active while you are in good health. Be grateful for your job. Exercise your free speech. This simple exercise can make the things you already have feel like a lot more.

In some cases, people suffer from anxiety related to the loss of these same types of things, but without the second key part of negative visualization: taking action. This exercise is pointless if you just create feelings of distress and sadness. You must find a way to us the negative energy of anxiety to push you forward into positive action. This way, if you do lose one of the valuable parts of your life, you will not feel that you wasted the time you had with it.

We may encounter another type of event, one that is sad or difficult and will inevitably happen. For example, most of us will experience the death of a parent at some point. It could also be a loved one with a terminal illness or a beloved pet with a life-span naturally much shorter than our own. It could also be something like our children growing up and leaving to start their own lives. For many people, these thoughts are quite distressing and may be the basis of anxiety-related intrusive thoughts.

Negative visualization encourages us to imagine these situations, as sad as they may be. Seneca, one of the ancient developers of Stoic thought, explained that "we should love all our dear ones...but always with the thought that we have no promise that we may keep them forever—nay, no promise even that we may keep them for long."

Negative visualization can thus help us realize that loss is a part of life and can prepare us for it so that we will, eventually, be OK. Perhaps life won't ever be the same, perhaps it will be harder, and perhaps it will be even better after a while, but we will find a way to continue.

In ancient times, in the absence of therapists and psychiatrists, philosophers acted as "physicians of the soul," and people turned to them for guidance. Stoicism was considered a powerful tool for mental well-being, especially in the Hellenic period, and philosophy was a necessity as counseling is today. It was accessible to everyone, and contrary to the perceptions of philosophy today, it was not about abstract wisdom. Stoicism offered simple, everyday solutions for everyday problems, and the practical concepts are popular to this day.

In ancient Greece, it was normal to seek help from a philosopher for mental health issues. Mental illnesses require remedies like any other, and ancient societies understood this better than we do. As we borrow their wisdom, we also need to embrace their sensibilities and world view when it comes to the malady and its treatment.

Given the similarity of CBT to Stoic philosophy, you could think of contemporary therapists as a type of philosopher, helping people understand themselves and the world around them in more realistic and effective ways. In this respect, their role hasn't changed much since the days of ancient Greece. The Greeks were concerned as much with the world as with the individual and how they related to each other. Today's cognitive behavioral therapists are part of that long legacy, helping to create harmony within the human mind in relation to the world. Of course, therapy has evolved over time, but its fundamentals have remained strikingly similar to ancient wisdom.

Step 6: The Behavioural Side of CBT

Behavioural Activation

Thus far, we've focused on the cognitive aspects of cognitive behavioural therapy. Behavioural changes are the other essential part of cognitive behavioural therapy. One strategy is known as behavioural activation, which aims to increase participation in pleasurable activities and events that improve mood. Especially for depression, avoidance of activities can worsen the condition by deepening isolation and reinforcing negative beliefs. This leads to increased avoidance in a vicious cycle. Behavioural activation can help break it.

For depression and other conditions, increasing activity can improve mood in multiple ways. First, it addresses avoidance coping mechanisms that deepen depression, anxiety, and phobias. Second, it can increase feelings of self-confidence, usefulness, and meaning by helping you engage in meaningful activities. Finally, by encouraging physical activity, it can bring about some of the physiological changes that improve mood. Surprisingly, engaging in these types of activities can improve mood even when you don't want to do them. To quote the Talmud, "One who seeks to improve, the way is opened for him."

Behavioural activation can include a wide range of activities, like exercising, meeting with friends, attending a club, and going to cultural or sporting events, as well as some essential life tasks like taking care of the home or doing taxes. Less pleasant activities like doing taxes or cleaning are important to improving mood through creating a sense of accomplishment and overcoming avoidance. For pleasant activities, behavioral activation can include a mixture of old and new.

Keep in mind that behavioral activation is different for anxiety and depression. For those suffering from low mood, avoidance of situations might be done out of a lack of energy or a belief that the person will not enjoy it. Thus, simply going to an event can improve mood by creating a feeling of accomplishment, even if the person did not like it and especially if he or she does enjoy it. For people with anxiety, avoidance may be due to fear of some aspect of the situation. In this case, behavioral activation can focus on physical activity and pleasant, meaningful activities that help reduce stress, while anxiety-inducing situations can be addressed with gradual exposure and a variety of other relaxation techniques.

The first step is identifying activities to include in your behavioral-activation plan. Focus first on pleasant activities. Think about hobbies and activities that you enjoyed in the past but stopped doing, things you do now but would like to do more of, and activities that you have never tried but think you would enjoy. You can also think about things that you would like to accomplish, rather than things that seem pleasant. Getting things done can be a powerful factor for mood improvement. Think about tasks that you need to do to improve your life, such as getting forms, bills, or paperwork in order, fixing things around the house, or making and going to appointments. Similarly, service activities like volunteering can help create a sense of usefulness and value to the community. The most important thing is finding activities that feel meaningful and important to you; otherwise you are unlikely to follow through.

Some possible ideas include:

- Spending time with friends or family or visiting neighbors
- Joining a club or group related to anything that interests you—language, film, politics, and so on
- Attending services at a place of worship
- Attending sporting events, concerts, or cultural events
- Getting a pet or playing with a friend's pet
- Going out to eat at a restaurant
- Doing yoga, meditation, or relaxation activities

- Doing puzzles, crosswords, or other brain games
- Spending time outside walking, biking, hiking, fishing, or gardening
- Getting physical activity in an enjoyable way—at a gym, at fitness classes, or at home
- Joining a recreational sports team
- Volunteering for a charity, school, faith group, arts organization, or environmental cause
- Taking lessons—music, art, cooking, language, martial arts, community education classes, and so on
- Doing hobbies on your own—reading, art, knitting, singing, outdoors, crafts, cars, and so on
- Doing home-improvement projects
- Doing tasks like taxes, renewing a license, and so on that give you a sense of accomplishment

The second step is setting goals and creating a plan for how you will incorporate these activities into your schedule. Select one to three activities that you would like to incorporate. Keep it to a reasonable amount of time per week, such as one longer activity every other day or a short daily activity. You can increase activities in the future if you feel more energetic or find ones you particularly enjoy. Then, assess how much time the activity will take, and figure out where it will work best in your schedule. Set a date in the near future to start the activity, and do it!

For example, you might wish to spend more time in nature, something you know you will enjoy. You could also begin volunteering at a soup kitchen in the neighborhood, something you wanted to do in the past. You may remember there is a large park ten minutes or so from your home. You could then call and find out that the soup kitchen needs volunteers for a two-hour time slot on Saturday mornings. You could decide that the best time to walk in the park is on the way home from work, and set aside half an hour on Monday, Wednesday, and Friday from 5:00 to 5:30 to walk. You might then confirm a volunteering time from 9:00 to 11:00 on Saturdays and agree to start next week.

As you make your plan, list obstacles and how you will overcome them. For example, if you have to work late sometimes and will miss an after-work group activity or a chance to take a bike ride, is there another time in the day or week that you can go? If not, come up with other activities that work better. There could also be issues of bad weather, traffic, family responsibilities, or other problems, but don't let these derail your plan. In addition, come up with a list of facilitators, or things that will encourage you to complete the activity. Perhaps you can call a friend to walk with you, as knowing that someone is expecting you will increase your chances of completing the activity. Or maybe your employer offers a reward program for physical activity. Maybe your spouse is especially supportive, and you can ask him or her to encourage you to attend a weekly club. Write down anything you think might be helpful. See the workbook in the appendix for a guide.

Ancient wisdom comes in handy even here. While developing a sense of gratitude helps free us from a delusional ego, doing charity enhances our self-worth. All the major religions provide the required motivation for altruism. It is important to give away a part of what you earn to the less fortunate. Hinduism, for instance, places additional emphasis on doing your dharma, or duty, and care for others. Generosity is one of the pillars of the spiritual path, and the benefits of this attribute have been substantiated by scientific research. When done over a period of time, charity makes the giver feel good about himself or herself, building self-esteem.

Graded Exposure

> *Nothing Either Good or Bad, But Thinking Makes It So*
> — Hamlet, Shakespeare

Another behavior-change strategy is called graded exposure, a way to learn how to face situations that make you feel stress or fear. This essentially means that you start with an activity that is relatively unstressful and become comfortable with it before building up to activities that are moderately stressful, and finally to ones that at first seemed highly stressful.

For example, let's say you're afraid of dogs, to the point where taking a walk in a city park is highly stressful. You would begin by making a list of activities related to dogs in order of how scary or anxiety-producing each one is, and then move down the list, allowing the anxiety to reduce by half before beginning the next activity. You might start by watching a documentary about dogs or viewing videos of friendly dogs online. Later you might go to a pet store and look at puppies. The following week you could ask to hold or play with a small puppy. Then you might call a friend with a calm, gentle dog and ask to spend some time with it in a controlled, relaxed situation. Over a period of weeks, you could call a friend with a more energetic dog, spend time watching dogs playing at a dog park, and finally, go to a dog park with a friend that owns a dog. You would repeat each of these activities several times per week, continuing the activity until anxiety peaked and receded, for as long as was needed to feel comfortable in the situation.

There are several important aspects of this process. First of all, it should be gradual. Choose a beginning activity that is relatively nonthreatening, and slowly work up to scarier situations. It should be a challenging but not traumatic process. Secondly, it's important to give yourself plenty of time in each situation to allow the anxiety to dissipate, rather than removing yourself from the situation before anxiety peaks. In this vein, make sure you avoid any distractions. In many cases, breathing exercises and music are helpful ways to deal with anxiety. In this case, though, the goal is to fully face the experience so that you can experience the anxiety and realize that it will diminish with time. The activity also needs to be repeated often, about three to five times per week, for full effectiveness. You can take as long as you need on each step, but try to move on to the next step once anxiety or fear has decreased by at least half.

Addressing Maladaptive Coping Mechanisms

Putting a stop to maladaptive coping mechanisms is another important behavioral dimension of CBT. As we've discussed, CBT encourages participation in activities that improve mood. Similarly, it discourages doing things that lead to lowered moods, either directly or indirectly. Sometimes people suffering from anxiety, depression, or other types of mental illness find coping mechanisms that make it easier to deal with the unpleasant feelings. Some coping mechanisms are fine and healthy; others are destructive. Some may also worsen anxiety or depression in the long term, even if they aren't directly harmful. For example, taking a brisk walk when you feel anxious could be a good coping mechanism. Avoiding situations that cause anxiety, such as giving presentations, may not harm you directly but will cause problems in the future by limiting your opportunities and worsening anxiety related to that situation. Drinking heavily when you feel anxious, on the other hand, is both directly and indirectly harmful and could lead to disastrous consequences.

Maladaptive coping mechanisms include:

- Drinking heavily or with the intention of dulling negative feelings

- Using illegal drugs
- Abusing prescription or over-the-counter medications
- Using other behaviors, such as sex or partying, to alter mood
- Mentally or emotionally disengaging from difficult situations
- Avoiding difficult situations
- Sleeping excessively
- Engaging in self-harm
- Having an eating disorder
- Engaging in excessive attention-seeking
- Being in denial
- Taking out anger, aggression, or frustration on people around you

In some cases, we keep doing behaviors that are harmful or that increase anxiety and depression in the long term because they provide some kind of short-term benefit. For example, drinking, drug use, or sex can provide some kind of escape for a person who is experiencing extreme stress in his or her life. Similarly, an eating disorder may provide a temporary sense of control for someone who feels that his or her life is out of control. It's important to think about what short-term benefits encourage you to continue these types of behaviors. Do they help you in some way or help you avoid something? Do they provide a rush or an escape? Do they get you attention or other things that feel good? Maladaptive behaviors like this are common, and having them doesn't mean you're a bad or weak person. Identifying these behaviors and why you do them helps you in two ways: it highlights the actions that need to be avoided and focuses you on the underlying problem that you need to address.

Stopping the use of maladaptive coping mechanisms can increase anxiety in the short term but ultimately helps reduce both anxious feelings and low mood. This is because continuing to avoid a stressful situation teaches your mind that avoidance equals reduced stress, and encourages you to be more afraid of it. If you face the situation, anxiety will peak but then decline as you realize that you are OK. The next time, the peak will be a little lower, and so on, until the situation feels manageable. However, if you avoid it each time, anxiety associated with the situation will remain high and even increase.

Step 7: Support CBT

Problem Solving

The eighth-century Indian Buddhist scholar Shantideva said, "If you *can* solve your problem, then what is the *need* of worrying: If you *can't* solve your problem, what is the *use* of worrying."

The goal of cognitive behavioral therapy is not to tell yourself that everything is OK and that there are no problems. There are, for all of us. Rather, the aim is to achieve a balanced, realistic view of different situations that allows us to react effectively and without excessive fear, anxiety, or low mood. While thought and belief challenging are useful when thoughts and beliefs are not true or when a situation is unchangeable, problem solving is good when a situation *is* changeable but may be fraught with anxiety. Problems may also be connected with depression, medical issues, addiction, or family issues. Some types of problems that could be addressed with this model include improving communication with your spouse, reducing your debt, dealing with a restriction imposed by illness, adhering to new diet, quitting smoking, getting to work on time, figuring out child care, or reducing the severity of disease symptoms.

This approach is not appropriate for all problems. If you are suffering from severe depression, problems that are mostly emotional, or serious mental illness, this approach is not adequate. In some cases, there isn't a solution in the sense that the problem will go away. The solution may be finding healthy coping mechanisms to be able to live with it. This is called emotion-focused coping and can help increase feelings of control and hopefulness and decrease stress. If this is the case, it may be more helpful to pursue a different method than problem solving.

The problem-solving approach taught with CBT has seven steps.

Step 1: Identify and describe the problem. The first step is describing the problem in detail. Write down what it is, the time frame, who it involves, where it happens, and so on. If you think your description might be exaggerated, you can use some of the evidence-for-or-against techniques to more accurately assess it. Choose a specific problem that is likely to have a concrete solution.

Step 2: Identify possible solutions. Brainstorm all possible solutions you can think of. Don't worry about the details at first, since even a ridiculous-sounding solution can lead you to a more realistic one. Think about the advice you might give a friend in this situation, or what you've done in similar situations. You can also ask others for advice. Keep an open mind.

Step 3: Evaluate possible solutions. Once you have a few possible solutions, write down the pros and cons of each one. In some cases, you may need professional advice from a doctor, lawyer, or administrator.

Step 4: Decide on optimal and backup solutions. Based on the pros and cons of the possible solutions, decide on the best solution and one or two backup solutions. Alternatively, you can simply rank the solutions in order of preference.

Step 5: Plan what you need to do. Plan out detailed steps needed to enact the solution you identified. Breaking it down into small steps can make it more approachable.

Step 6: Carry out your plan. Do the steps you listed in Step 5. If needed, shift to one of your backup plans.

Step 7: Review and adjust plan as needed. How did it go? Is the problem solved or reduced to a manageable level? If the problem is not solved or if a new problem has arisen, you can return to Step 1 and formulate a new solution and plan. See the workbook in the appendix for a guide.

Healthy Lifestyle

Sleep

There are things you can do in your life outside the CBT strategies that can greatly benefit your well-being and increase the effectiveness of any therapy you use. One of the most important factors is sleep. Getting enough sleep is important for mood, energy levels, physical health, and even the chemical balance of the brain. Things like anxiety can make it harder to sleep, creating a reinforcing cycle of stress and exhaustion. However, there are many simple changes you can make to help yourself get a good night's sleep:

- Try to sleep and get up at the same time every day and to sleep when you feel tired.
- Don't oversleep by more than an hour to make up for lost sleep.
- Don't watch TV, use electronics, or eat in bed.
- Give yourself thirty minutes to an hour before bed to relax.
- Avoid napping more than twenty minutes during the day if it makes it hard to sleep at night.
- Not everyone needs eight hours of sleep per night. Focus on getting restful sleep, rather than getting "enough" sleep, which can lead to more anxiety.
- Make sure that your bedroom is quiet, dark,

comfortable, and free from distractions.

- Avoid caffeine, alcohol, and nicotine in the four hours before going to bed, or avoid them entirely if you find that you are sensitive to their effects.
- Get physical activity during the day, but not late in the evening.
- Ask your doctor about the side effects of medications—some can lead to trouble sleeping.

Healthy Eating

Many people also find that a healthier diet contributes to a better sense of overall well-being. It can also contribute to weight loss and improvement of other health factors, relieving anxiety in the process. If you feel that addressing your diet now would lead to more anxiety, leave it for a later time. However, if you feel motivated to improve your diet, go for it. It could be an effective way to feel healthier and less anxious or depressed.

The Mediterranean and DASH (Dietary Approaches to Stop Hypertension) diets are some of the best supported in terms of scientific literature, and both can be delicious, flexible, and sustainable in the long term. Outside specific approaches, you can simply aim to eat more fruits, vegetables, whole grains, fish, healthy fats like olive oil and avocado, nuts, and seeds, and less red meat, high-fat dairy, white flour and refined grains, sugars, hydrogenated oils, and processed foods in general. If you enjoy cooking, taking cooking classes and making healthier home-cooked meals could be a great part of your behavioral-activation strategy.

Physical Activity

In the section on behavioral activation, we mentioned physical activity as a way to improve mood. Physical activity does not have to mean exercise. Many people believe that they must go to the gym and run on a treadmill or ride a stationary bike for it to count. This is not at all true! There are many enjoyable ways to be active that don't take you anywhere near a gym. Walking, biking, and hiking outside can be fun and relaxing, and research shows that a brisk walk can be just as helpful as a run for improving long-term health. Winter sports like skiing and skating are great too. Low-intensity activities like gardening, playing catch with your child, doing yard work, or actively cleaning the house count as well.

Mantra Meditation

Meditation is a great way to relieve stress and cultivate mindfulness. There are many approaches, but one easy way to begin is mantra meditation. It is a form of meditation in which one chooses a sound or phrase and repeats it anywhere from a few to hundreds of times. It can be as simple as a soothing sound, such as "om" or "ahh," or it can be a phrase in any language expressing sentiments of compassion, kindness, or peace. You can make one up yourself or use a traditional ancient mantra that has been murmured for centuries. There is really great flexibility in mantra meditation, making this powerful technique all the more approachable.

Choosing a Mantra

Simple mantras can be soothing and help you clear your mind during meditation, and compassionate phrases can give you a chance to fully absorb the message. We will suggest several traditional mantras to get you started, and then provide suggestions for how to create your own.

The most well-known mantra is also the simplest: *om*. Hindu, Jain, and other traditions teach that it is the original sound of the universe and that it has a deep spiritual power signifying the three characteristics of divine energy: creation, preservation, and liberation. Regardless of the beliefs associated with it, the om mantra has uniquely soothing qualities. The sounds feel natural and produce a calming vibration that supports both mental and physical relaxation.

When chanting the om mantra, you'll really be making three sounds. Begin with an "ah" sound; then let it shift into an "oo." At the end, close your lips to make the humming "mmm" sound. This last one should resonate throughout your chest. You can hold each sound for as long as you like and then pause briefly before repeating. You can expand on the om mantra by chanting "om shanti, shanti, shanti," which means "om peace, peace, peace."

Another simple mantra is *Sat nam*, which translates to "Truth is my name." The "saaat" portion is pronounced for eight to thirty-five times as long as the "nam" portion, resulting in a resonance in the chest that, much like om, is calming.

A slightly longer option with the same sort of calming effect is *Ra ma da sa, sa say so hung*. It means "Sun, moon, earth, infinity—all that is in infinity, I am thee." Traditionally, this mantra is accompanied by a specific pose. Sit comfortably and press your upper arms against your sides. Bend your elbows at a ninety-degree angle, and turn your palms to face upward. Kundalini yoga practitioners believe that this mantra and pose are restorative and send healing energy to the self and others.

A good option for a simple, traditional compassionate mantra is *Lokah samastah sukhino bhavantu*. It is pronounced "low-kah sa-ma-stah soo-ki-no ba-van-too" and roughly translates to "May all beings everywhere be happy and free." A quick Internet search will turn up dozens of videos offering help with pronunciation or simply repeating the mantra multiple times as a meditation aid.

A slightly longer mantra expressing good wishes toward other is as follows:

Sarvesham svastir bhavatu (ser-vay-sham sva-steer ba-va-too)

Sarvesham shantir bhavatu (ser-vay-sham shan-teer ba-va-too)

Sarvesham purnam bhavatu (ser-vay-sham puur-nam ba-va-too)

Sarvesham mangalam bhavatu (ser-vay-sham mang-ga-lam ba-va-too)

It expresses a wish for well-being for all, peace for all, wholeness for all, and happiness for all. Again, you can find many videos online that can help you get the hang of chanting by searching for this phrase.

If none of these mantras resonate with you, or if you'd just like to make something more personal, you can create your own mantra. It can be as simple as a sound—play around with making different "ahh," "eee," and "hmmm" sounds until you find one that feels soothing and calming. To create a compassionate mantra, first think of the sentiment you want to express. It could be related to loving-kindness and acceptance toward yourself and others, wishes for peace, or anything else you want to remind yourself of. Then, try to find words that fit the meaning and that are easy and pleasant to say many times in a row. Work on paper if you find it helpful, or simply say the words aloud. Things like "love for all beings" or "peace within and without" could work. Once you've chosen a mantra, you can begin the meditation!

Beginning Mantra Meditation

First, choose a quiet, comfortable place where you won't be interrupted. Sit on a couch, comfortable chair, or yoga mat, lie on your bed, or lean against a pillow. If you're sitting on the ground, you can make it more comfortable by sitting on a small pillow or folded blanket so that you can keep your back straight and let your knees fall gently outward. Place your hands on your thighs, or press them lightly together in front of you. Avoid bright lights, as they can be overly stimulating.

Focus on your breathing. Breathe in a deep and relaxed manner, but don't try to control the breath. Breathe naturally. Start by focusing on your intention. It could be something like deepening self-compassion, increasing kindness to others, or letting go. Many people find that choosing an intention for their meditation session helps them stay focused and brings it deeper meaning.

Begin chanting your sound or phrase. If you have chosen a traditional Sanskrit mantra, you can find guides online to help with pronunciation, but this isn't the most important thing. Simply chant with a tone and speed that feels comfortable.

Draw your attention to the vibrations created by the mantra. This will be particularly noticeable with the om mantra, which you should be able to feel throughout your chest and belly. If thoughts come to your mind, gently let them go. It is normal to feel distracted or frustrated during meditation sometimes. There is no perfection to be achieved—it is enough to simply try. Repeat the chant for a few minutes. You can continue chanting for as long as you wish, or shift to silent meditation.

For those who follow a faith, repetitive contemplation of any prayer or passage from scripture can be effective as well. Choose any passage from your holy book and chant it again and again silently, all the while paying attention to the words. Enjoy each word and every phrase. Listen to yourself as you recite the passage. What insights and reflections does it awaken in you? Watch your response to this prayer.

And when you finish, spend a few seconds by yourself in divine silence.

To get the full benefits of meditation, it's recommended to do it every day. Try to set aside ten to fifteen minutes each day to do mantra meditation of another kind. If you can't, that's OK—just do the best you can. "Headspace" is a helpful place to start. You can try their *Take Ten* course for free. Read about the benefits of meditation by visiting www.Headspace.com or find them in the App store.

Nature Therapy

Recent studies have found that interacting with nature on a regular basis has a tremendous impact on our sense of health, happiness, and well-being. This is especially true for creative, rather than knowledge-based, interaction. You don't have to be working or trail running, just meandering along a path, sitting in a pretty clearing, or sketching something you find beautiful. One of the biggest impacts is on stress levels. In a 2014 study titled "The Influence of Urban Green Environments on Stress Relief Measures: A Field Experiment," researchers in Finland concluded that short visits to woodlands or urban parks measurably increased positive feelings and led participants to feel restored, while decreasing stress and levels of cortisol.

A 2015 study titled "The Benefits of Nature Experience:

Improved Affect and Cognition" also found evidence that spending time in nature makes people happier and less anxious. The researchers divided subjects into two groups and had them walk for fifty minutes in a busy urban area or in a woodland. The people who walked in a natural area had better moods and scored lower on measures of anxiety and rumination than people who walked in urban areas. In addition, the nature-walk group showed improved scores on tests measuring working memory performance!

These recent studies are supported by research from over twenty-five years ago. In a 1991 study titled "Stress Recovery during Exposure to Natural and Urban Environments," the authors found that after participants were shown a stressful video, they relaxed much more quickly when shown a second video featuring natural scenes than when the second video featured urban scenes. Research also shows that experiencing nature results in stronger parasympathetic nervous system activity, a sign of relaxation. Two great ways to maximize the benefits are forest bathing and bird-watching.

Forest Bathing

A simple way to engage with nature has been named "forest bathing" by researchers in Japan. Forest bathing means spending time in a forest and focusing completely on relaxation. It's not about hiking or counting steps, though you certainly can meander along a trail; rather, it's about letting go of the rest of the world and enjoying being in nature. Forest bathing has been studied extensively in Japan and is now an official part of national public health campaigns. Researchers found that it results in lower heart rates, blood pressure, and levels of the stress hormone cortisol. People also have improved scores on assessments measuring hostility and depression.

Forest bathing is easy to do. If you live near a forest, such as a state or national park, set aside an hour or two for a visit. If not, you can get many of the same benefits from a city park with trees and green space. It doesn't specifically have to be a forest either. A meadow, a prairie, a river, or any outside area you find beautiful and soothing will do.

Make a point to immerse yourself in the experience. Turn off your phone, or leave it at home. Engage all your senses in the experience: notice the smell of the soil, the air, and plants; the sounds of wind, water, and animals; the texture of leaves and bark; and the feel of the earth beneath your feet. Enjoy the bright colors and the many shades of green, brown, blue, and gray that make up natural landscapes. Ponder the diversity of the flora and fauna and how they interact and depend on one another. Look for signs of animal life. If you visit the same place often, notice how it changes through the seasons.

Bird-Watching

Bird-watching is a wonderful way to feel totally immersed in the experience of being outside, since you are focused on each flash of color and light and every rustle and call. It's exactly this kind of complete interaction with nature that helps relieve stress and boost mood. It also leads to a sense of wonder about the natural world, as you develop an appreciation for the different types of birds and their unique habits.

If you're already a birder, make a point to go out a least a few times per month. Visit new locations, and pay attention to seasonal migrations that may give you a chance to see new birds. Birding is also a great activity to organize trips and vacations around, since many beautiful natural areas around the world boast diverse bird life and cater to birders.

Even if you have never gone birding before, it is an easy hobby to take up. All you need are a pair of binoculars and some way to find out about bird species in your area—a guidebook, the web, or a knowledgeable friend. Head to a park, a green space, or even a large backyard, and see how many different types you can find. Depending on where you live, you might be able to attract a wide variety of birds with feeders. You can also look up a local chapter of the Audubon Society, the American Birding Association, or one of the many local organizations to find birding walks and trips.

The Power of Awe

Awe is often fleeting and hard to define, but we can think of it as the sense of amazement, wonder, and surprise we feel when observing something beyond our normal experience of the world, something beautiful, deeply moving, or transcendent. Awe is often unexpected, mysterious, and evocative of a sense of vastness. It usually requires us to alter or refine our understanding of the world, which is why it has the potential to change our feelings, styles of thinking, and actions. Many things can inspire awe, including nature, spirituality, art, and music.

Researchers recently found that experiencing a sense of awe makes people kinder, more altruistic, less focused on themselves, and less anxious. In a paper titled "Awe, the Small Self, and Prosocial Behavior," published in June 2015, the authors suggested that experiencing awe may actually have an important social function. In a series of experiments, they asked participants about how often they felt awe, showed them videos, and had them participate in activities designed to inspire a range of different emotions, including awe, pride, and fear. People who reported feeling awe more often and people who watched the awe-inspiring videos were more generous in follow-up experiments.

The Big Value of Feeling Small

Part of the value of awe is that it makes you feel small, in a good way. This isn't the same as feeling small as a result of discrimination, cruelty, or powerlessness. That kind of small usually means that you have been made to feel meaningless or less valuable than other people, and that's a terrible feeling to have. The good kind of feeling small is universal—we are *all* tiny in the great scheme of things, and that means that our problems are tiny too. Our lives are fables in a boundless cosmic story.

Disorders like anxiety and depression tend to make us extremely focused on our own lives and problems. We may become overly focused on ourselves. This often comes from a sense overwhelm—the feeling that we are unable to deal with our current reality. This can result in emotional paralysis in the face of things that aren't truly threatening. Our individual worlds become stressful and demand more and more of our attention. However, it doesn't mean that we are truly selfish or we don't care about others—you are certainly not a "bad person" for feeling like this! Overwhelm is a common symptom of many mental illnesses and disorders. This intense self-focus is a form of suffering caused by anxiety or depression, and not simply a sign of selfishness. In fact, we usually care deeply about our loved ones and feel bad that we are not as responsive or caring as we would like to be. It becomes isolating, and isolation is torturous for humans. Humans are naturally social creatures: we enjoy the sense of belonging, we tend to seek identities as part of a group, and we care deeply about connections with others, as well as their well-being. Being in an emotional state in which it is difficult to connect with or help people is thus quite distressing.

Gaining perspective on your problems, breaking out of this self-focused thinking style, and finding ways to feel small (the good kind) are as much about helping you as they are about helping others. One way to do this is by having awe-inspiring experiences.

Nature

We've already talked about some of the benefits of being in nature for stress reduction. Nature is also powerful source of awe-inspiring moments: experiencing beautiful sunsets, mountains, waterfalls, crashing waves, stunning coastlines, giant trees, and wondrous animal life can make you feel both small and wonderfully connected to the rest of the living world. Pondering the fact that the mountains you're standing on have been there for millions of years, that the tree towering above you is made up of tiny cells distantly related to your own, or that the birds stopping to rest in your backyard inherently know how to migrate thousands of miles can provide perspective and shift your focus away from aspects of your life that you perceive as negative.

Seek out these experiences as much as possible. If you have vacation time, make a point to go somewhere with natural beauty, whether it's on the other side of the world or just an hour away at a nature reserve. If you like adventure activities, do something exhilarating in a beautiful place, like skiing, mountain biking, paragliding, or windsurfing. Walking, hiking, cycling, horseback riding, or just relaxing in the presence of stunning natural features can help you experience a sense of awe and put things in perspective.

Watching a visually stunning documentary can also inspire a sense of awe about the natural world. Though cool nature facts alone can be quite interesting and sometimes awesome, great narration paired with incredible cinematography tends to be more moving. Try the Planet

Earth series from BBC (2007), the Disneynature film *Earth* (2007), *Winged Migration* (2001), *Oceans* (2009), *Hidden Kingdoms* (2014), or the Blue Planet series (2001). In addition, as the 1991 study we mentioned above found, just watching nature scenes can have a positive impact on mood and stress levels.

Stargazing Therapy

Another accessible way of putting things in perspective is staring up at the night sky. BJ Miller, a triple amputee who went on to become a world-renowned palliative care physician, has this reflection about therapeutic stargazing: "Realize that we're all on the same planet at the same time. Realize that the light hitting your eye is ancient, stars that you're seeing may no longer exist by the time the light gets to you. Just mulling the bare-naked facts of the cosmos is enough to put all my neurotic anxieties in their proper place."

Ed Cooke, a British entrepreneur and grandmaster of memory, has a similar thought: "Imagine the world from the stars. Then you zoom in and you're like, 'There's this tiny little character there for a fragment of time worrying about X.'"

You may also enjoy Carl Sagan's famous "Pale Blue Dot" video—simply search for that title online, and several videos will come up. It is a wonderful meditation on the tininess of earth and humanity, both humbling and moving.

Spirituality

Too often, spirituality gets overly muddled up with organized religion. These two are not the same thing. All humans have a spiritual capacity and inclination, and it has nothing to do with stating certain beliefs, deferring to a man with a special outfit, or reading a specific book. Spirituality is our innate sense of wonder about our origins, our desire to question and ponder and reflect on the meaning of it all, and our ability and willingness to transcend the material world and our physical wants in search of something that feels more profound.

Whatever your faith or religion—or lack of such—your spirituality can be a source of awe. Many people—philosophers, scientists, and artists—who did or do not identify as religious have spent their lives studying the world and the human condition and been deeply moved by it. Take a bit of time each day to reflect on something awesome: The human capacity for love. The complex and diverse yet biologically unified nature of life. *The fact that life exists at all!* The vastness of the universe and the relative tininess of earth. Our ability to think abstractly, make art, and appreciate beauty. The fact that human bodies house more bacteria than human cells and need them to flourish. The fact that 96 percent of the universe is made of dark matter and we don't really know what that is. The fact that stories written thousands of years ago can still make us laugh and cry. Whatever it is that makes you say "wow," stop and think about it for a while.

For people who do follow a certain belief system, many teachings may inspire awe. A wonderful thing about Buddhism, philosophical Taoism, and some branches of other religions is that they offer awe-inspiring ideas, reflections, and explanations to anyone, regardless of a person's beliefs. Spirituality is, of course, highly personal, so it will be up to you to seek out verses from specific holy texts, commentaries, rituals, or sermons that you find awe inspiring. If you already practice a religion or faith that you find meaningful, we encourage you to go deeper in search of transcendent wisdom or experiences. Find a scholar, teacher, priest, imam, or minister that you respect, and ask him or her for advice.

Art and Music

The beauty and depth of human expression through art and music can be moving and awe inspiring. Listen to singers whose voices you find truly unique and beautiful. Put on an opera or a symphony with a fabulous, sweeping finale. Look at paintings and sculptures that are stunning in their aesthetic, technique, or capture of emotion. Read poetry that touches you with its sincerity and creativity. If no artists or artworks come to mind right away, that's perfectly OK. Think of art and music as a therapeutic path to explore, with the goal of discovering a few creations that inspire a transformative sense of awe.

Here are a few ideas to get you started:

- the stunningly lifelike marble sculptures of Gian Lorenzo Bernini
- the Chauvet cave paintings, made thirty thousand years ago
- the Lascaux cave paintings, made about seventeen thousand years ago
- the uniquely blocky, colorful, and perceptive paintings of Paul Cézanne
- Vincent van Gogh's *Starry Night* and other works
- Auguste Rodin's passion-filled bronze and marble sculptures
- the detail and humanity conveyed in Leonardo da Vinci's paintings and drawings
- *Girl with a Pearl Earring,* by Johannes Vermeer
- Claude Monet's messy-up-close-but-perfect-from-afar impressionist works

- Mayan pyramids in the Yucatán peninsula
- King Tut's funerary mask
- the hauntingly beautiful choral piece "O Magnum Mysterium"

Writing about Awe

One of the easiest ways to experience feelings of awe anytime is to write about a past experience you had. Remembering an awe-inspiring experience in detail creates similar feelings in the present. It's simple: Choose a memory such as a moving concert or performance, beautiful scenery from a trip, an incredible act of kindness or generosity that you observed, a profound spiritual experience, or even something like the best meal you ever ate if it really surprised you! Then, write it down in as much detail as possible. What exactly touched you about that experience? The sounds? The sights? Perhaps the taste and smell? The emotions it created? An important realization that the experience led you to have? Spend ten to fifteen minutes noting down everything that comes to mind. If you like, designate a special "awe book," in which you write down past awe-inspiring experiences and new ones as they happen. This will help you keep a sense of awe constantly fresh and available.

Additional Reading

Therapists who use cognitive behavioral therapy usually assign readings for clients to complete at home. You can do this too by selecting relevant books from the list below and reading a few pages per day. This list is by no means exclusive—there are many resources for CBT in print and online.

- Dennis Greenberger and Christine A. Padesky, *Mind over Mood: Change the Way You Feel by Changing the Way You Think* (1995)
- David Burns, *The Feeling Good Handbook* (1999)
- Davies William, *Overcoming Anger and Irritability: A Self-Help Guide to Using Cognitive Behavioral Therapy* (2000)
- Susan Jeffers, *Feel the Fear and Do It Anyway* (2007)
- Helen Kennelly, *Overcoming Anxiety* (2009)
- Charles Young, *Introduction to Coping with Health Anxiety* (2007)
- Melanie Fennel, *Overcoming Low Self-Esteem: A Self-Help Guide Using Cognitive Behavioral Therapy* (1999)
- Paul Gilbert, *Overcoming Depression: A Self-Help Guide Using Cognitive Behavioral Techniques* (2007)
- Brenda Hogan, *Introduction to Coping with Phobias*

(2007)

- Frances Cole, *Overcoming Chronic Pain: A Self-Help Guide Using Cognitive Behavioral Techniques* (2005)
- Derrick Silove, *Overcoming Panic & Agoraphobia: A Self-Help Guide Using Cognitive Behavioral Techniques* (2009)
- Gillian Butler, *Overcoming Social Anxiety and Shyness* (1999)

Conclusion

Anxiety and low mood are common problems faced by a majority of people at some point in their lifetimes. Happily, cognitive behavioral therapy offers an approachable, flexible method to deal with these struggles. We hope this book has been a helpful introduction to applying CBT techniques on your own. Now that you understand the basic approach of cognitive behavioral therapy, you can get started today. As we've discussed, it can be broken down into seven steps:

- Step 1: Identify the problem.
- Step 2: Set goals.
- Step 3: Identify obstacles.
- Step 4: Challenge automatic and intrusive thoughts.
- Step 5: Identify and challenge assumptions and core beliefs.
- Step 6: Use behavioral modification strategies.
- Step 7: Support CBT with problem solving, a healthy lifestyle, and additional reading.

The whole process will take at least a few weeks, and it can be used over your whole life. But you can do at least three steps today! If you have thirty minutes right now, you can identify the problem, set goals, and begin to think about obstacles. You can always come back to it tomorrow and make changes. If you have a little more time, you can even start identifying automatic thoughts. The worksheets on the following pages are a great way to get started.

We wish you the best in learning how to find peace in the midst of whatever challenges life may bring you.

> *"Retain faith that you will prevail in the end, regardless of the difficulties, and at the same time confront the most brutal facts of your current reality, whatever they might be."*
> — James Stockdale

Appendix A: Cognitive Behavioural Therapy Workbook

First, **identify the problem,** how often it occurs, how intensely you experience it, and how it impacts your life.

Problem:

....

....

Frequency:

....

Severity:

....

Impact:

....

....

Write down your goals as specifically as possible, including a time frame.

Goal 1:

....

....

Goal 2:

....

....

Goal 3:

....

....

Goal 4:

....

....

Identify obstacles that you affect your progress and how you can address them.

Obstacle:...

Strategy 1:

....

....

Strategy 2:

....

....

Strategy 3:

....

....

Obstacle:...

Strategy 1:

....

....

Strategy 2:

....

....

Strategy 3:

....

....

Obstacle:...

Strategy 1:

....

....

Strategy 2:

....

....

Strategy 3:

....

....

After reading the section on **cognitive distortions**, write down what types you tend to make so you can be more aware of them:

....

....

....

....

....

....

....

....

....

....

....

....

Thought Record – Identifying Automatic Thoughts

Situation (what, where, who, why, when…)	Emotion and intensity (0-100)	Automatic thoughts (cognitive distortions?)

Thought Record – Challenging Automatic Thoughts

Automatic thought	Evidence for	Evidence against	Alternative thought + new mood rating

Choose two to three activities for the behavioral-activation portion of CBT.

Activity:

....

When:

....

Obstacles: ....

....

....

Facilitators: ....

....

....

Activity:

....

When:

....

Obstacles: ....

....

....

Facilitators: ....

....

....

Activity:

………………………………………………………………………………

When:

………………………………………………………………………………

Obstacles: ………………………………..……………………………

………………………………………………………………

……………………………………..…………………………

Facilitators: ……………………………………………………………

…………………………………………………………………

…………………………………………………………………

Progress Chart

Mood & intensity	Activities completed	Progress toward goals
Morning: Mid-Day: Evening:		
Morning: Mid-Day: Evening:		
Morning: Mid-Day: Evening:		
Morning: Mid-Day: Evening:		
Morning: Mid-Day: Evening:		
Morning: Mid-Day: Evening:		
Morning: Mid-Day: Evening:		

Problem Solving

What is the problem?

……………………………………………………………………………

……………………………………………………………………………

……………………………………………………………………………

What are some possible solutions?

……………………………………………………………………………

……………………………………………………………………………

……………………………………………………………………………

What are the advantages and disadvantages of each?

Solution 1 pros:

……………………………………………………………………………

Solution 1 cons:

……………………………………………………………………………

Solution 2 pros:

……………………………………………………………………………

Solution 2 cons:

……………………………………………………………………………

Solution 3 pros:

……………………………………………………………………………

Solution 3 cons:

……………………………………………………………………………

What is the optimal solution? What is the second best choice?

……………………………………………………………………………

……………………………………………………………………………

What do you need to do, exactly, to do the optimal solution and the backup option if needed?

....

....

....

....

....

What happened? Did your solution address the problem? What more needs to be done now?

....

....

....

....

....

....

....

....

....

....

....

....

....

....

Appendix B: The Six-Step Formula for Peace of Mind

1. Pause

Take control by pausing immediately after the stimulus or event (not reacting). Listen to your thoughts without analyzing them—do not try to think your way out. Instead, connect with the energy of your thoughts—feel your way out. Gently come back to the reality of the present moment. Remember that meaning and significance are added by you and your mind, so be careful not to make hurried assumptions. Slow down.

2. Note

Dispassionately note the thought for what it is: anger, sadness, joy, contentment, disgust, embarrassment, amusement, and so on. We are now training the mind to be more aware. This helps separate your identity from your changing moods and mental chatter (by becoming the observer instead of the thinker). Remember that even the most difficult times will surely pass. As a reminder, say to yourself, "This too will pass."

3. Zero identification

Embrace thoughts as real but not necessarily true. Accept your experience without resistance. But don't get caught in the trap of feeling identical with thoughts. Remember that we generate anywhere between twenty thousand and seventy thousand thoughts per day. Realize that anyone can experience any thought, kind or cruel. If you ever feel overwhelmed by irrational thinking, say to yourself, "Real, but not true."

"I," "mine," and "myself"—these are just added thoughts. The more identified with thoughts we become, the more intense and personal they feel. Reflect on what's beautiful and beneficial in your life; accept and let go of what's unhelpful or afflictive.

4. Rational permission

Give yourself rational permission to let go of unpleasant thoughts. Be strong and deliberate. Commit to moving beyond your mental chatter. Remember it is you who holds the keys to your mind. You decide what is meaningful and what is not. (This is especially important if you feel attached to an old, unhelpful interpretation.)

5. Abandoning negative thoughts

Completely let go of negative thoughts. Be pragmatic and compassionate to yourself. Detach. Let go of compulsive thinking, again and again. Abandon thoughts that do not benefit you or others. Accept but refuse to indulge negative thoughts, and you will quickly feel in control again. Practice wise detachment, and thoughts will not control you.

6. Diligent practice

Finally, simply repeat the process of "notice and let go" if rumination continues. This process literally rewires your brain. It forges a healthy relationship between you and your thoughts. You will no longer feel identified with unhelpful thoughts. Now you are truly free!

The Freedom Equation

Full-Engagement + Non-Attachment

=

Freedom!

Made in the USA
Lexington, KY
01 February 2018